ECOTOURISM AND BIODIVERSITY CONSERVATION

ECONOMIC ISSUES, PROBLEMS AND PERSPECTIVES

Additional books in this series can be found on Nova's website
under the Series tab.

Additional E-books in this series can be found on Nova's website
under the E-books tab.

TOURISM AND HOSPITALITY DEVELOPMENT AND MANAGEMENT

Additional books in this series can be found on Nova's website
under the Series tab.

Additional E-books in this series can be found on Nova's website
under the E-books tab.

ECONOMIC ISSUES, PROBLEMS AND PERSPECTIVES

ECOTOURISM AND BIODIVERSITY CONSERVATION

Suresh C. Rai

Nova Science Publishers, Inc.
New York

Library of Congress Cataloging-in-Publication Data

Rai, Suresh Chand, 1958-
  Ecotourism and biodiversity conservation / Suresh C. Rai.
      p. cm.
  Includes bibliographical references and index.
  ISBN 978-1-61324-242-1 (softcover)
  1. Ecotourism. 2. Biodiversity conservation. I. Title.
  G156.5.E26R45 2011
  333.95--dc22
                            2011009054

Published by Nova Science Publishers, Inc. ✝ *New York*

ABOUT THE AUTHOR

Dr. Suresh C. Rai received his M. Sc. Degree in 1979 and his Ph.D. degree in 1984 from The Banaras Hindu University, Varanasi, Department of Geography is teaching physical geography at the Department of Geography, Delhi School of Economics, University of Delhi since 2005. Before joining University of Delhi he worked as Senior Scientist in G.B. Pant Institute of Himalayan Environment and Development (An Autonomous Institute under Ministry of Environment and Forests, Government of India) at its Sikkim and North-East Unit and conducted research work on Integrated Watershed Management, Carbon Dynamics and Ecotourism aspects. He was recipient of Honorable Mention Best Paper Award, 1998 from Soil and Water Conservation Society, USA. His principal area of research is watershed management, mountain hydrology and ecotourism and biodiversity conservation of Himalaya. He has published over 65 research papers in refereed scientific journals and authored/edited 4 books.

PREFACE

Tourism is the most important non-farm activity in the mountainous region. In mountain belts the aesthetic value of the land is by itself one of the critical assets for the otherwise impoverished communities. The growth of population and the increasing demand at the individual level of various non-farm items have expanded the demand of goods beyond the traditional technological practices of mountain community and their cultural sensitivities. These initiatives of the Government have only mirrored Western models of tourism development rather than developing appropriate, need-based strategies for harnessing the potential.

Ecotourism is currently a "hot" topic. It is a movement that potentially involves billion of dollars, and conservation of biological diversity. The tourism industry is booming with new nature trips, dubbed ecotourism. Travelers are visiting parks and reserves worldwide like never before and are looking to understand and appreciate the natural environment. Protected area managers are facing increasing number of visitors to parks and biosphere reserves. Ecotourism offers many unique challenges and opportunities to protected area and tourism managers. The economic valuation of cultural goods and services has gained increasing interest from policy makers and cultural economists.

The present study has been divided into five chapters. Chapter one deals with an introductory outline of the ecotourism and biodiversity conservation, biodiversity valuation and tourism policy. Since not much study has been carried out on the topic in the Indian context, more attention is paid to review studies carried out in other countries. Chapter two is devoted to describe the biodiversity status and significance on global, regional and local level. The chapter on growth and impact of tourism (third chapter) deals with tourism growth, tourism pressure, nature and pattern of adventure/trekking travel, visitor's opinion and reaction, and tourism impacts. It is followed by economic valuation (Chapter four).

Participatory planning and biodiversity conservation has been discussed in chapter fifth.

The author would like to thank individuals, organizations, and academic institutions whose research publications, technical reports, annual reports and books provided the much needed information for developing the text, tables and figures. Author thankfully acknowledges all the original sources of information and the concerned publishers.

The author wish to acknowledge all those who have helped and provided useful input into this work such as Dr. A.K. Saha for his unending support, right suggestions, and constant encouragement throughout this work. I am thankful to the Head, Department of Geography, Delhi School of Economics, University of Delhi for providing the necessary facilities. I am highly grateful to Dr. P.R. Mondal, Department of Anthropology, University of Delhi for his valuable suggestions. The author also wishes to acknowledge all those who have helped and provided useful input into this work.

I am thankful to Prof. J.S. Singh, FNA (Retd.), Department of Botany, Banaras Hindu University and Prof. K.M.M. Dakshini (Retd.), Department of Botany, Delhi University for their visionary ideas and time to time suggestions. I am especially indebted to all my family members for their constant support.

Suresh C. Rai

CONTENTS

LIST OF TABLES

List of Tables (Continued)

LIST OF FIGURES

Chapter 1

INTRODUCTION

1.1. BACKGROUND

Throughout human history, people have moved in and out of their areas. While mountain regions are the centres of society in many tropical and sub-tropical countries. Individuals and groups of people from both lowland and mountain settlements have also temporarily visited higher areas in the mountains for various resources such as minerals, timber, or summer pastures or to visit holy places. Since the last century, and increasingly from the 1950s, significant flows of people into the mountains have taken place. The majority come for religious pilgrimage and leisure, contributing to the world's largest industry (Price, et al. 1997).

The term "tourist" meaning "an individual who travels for the pleasure of travelling, out of curiosity" made it first appearance around 1800 (Ceballos-Lascurian, 1996). But the origins of this activity go back considerably further. In the 18th and 19th centuries, the "Grand Tour" became extremely fashionable among the European aristocrats for adventure and discovery as the new motivations for travel. However, tourism did not become more accessible to the population in general until the time of the Industrial revolution (Wood and House, 1991). During this time, a considerable amount of travel for pleasure was essentially a quest for spectacular scenery. This was the beginning of travel for pleasure and of the transformation of travel into tourism. The era of organized tourism had started its journey.

Early part of this century by the time summer holidays were taken regularly by European and American, the improvements in international and intra-national tourist facilities, especially the introduction of chartered flights, increasing cheaper and varied tourist attractions have further stimulated and provided essential conditions for the growth of tourism. However, by this time, tourism started to earn itself a very bad name due to thoughtless development, and disruption of local cultures, values and economics (Maharana, 2000). Since the Second World War, the growth of international tourism has been phenomenal. Annual tourists arrivals worldwide increased from 25 million in 1950 to 450 million in 1990 (Christ et al. 2003).

Today tourism is often described as the world's "biggest" industry on the basis of its contribution to global gross domestic product (GDP), the number of jobs it generates, and the number of clients it serves (Box 1).

Box 1. The World Biggest Industry

Statistics produced by the World Travel and Tourism Council (WTTC) indicate that tourism generates 11% of global GDP, employs 200 million people, and transports nearly 700 million international travelers per year- a figure that is expected to double by 2020 (Christ, et al. 2003).
According to the World Tourism Organization, international tourism:
• Accounts for 36% of trade in commercial services in advanced economies and 66% in developing economies;
• Constitute 3-10% of GDP in advanced economies and up to 40% in developing economies;
• Generated US$ 464 billion in tourism receipts in 2001;
• Is one of the top five exports for 83% of countries and the main source of foreign currency for at least 38% of countries?

Tourism has rapidly won recognition as an activity generating a number of social and economic benefits like promotion of national integration and international understanding, creation of employment opportunities, removal of regional imbalances, opening of new growth centre, augmenting of foreign exchange earnings, thus redressing the balance of payments situation (Singh, 1986). It is significant that many of these beneficial aspects of domestic and international tourism have special relevance to socio-economic development. It is a smokeless industry of great importance. Tourism is traveling for predominantly recreational or leisure purposes or the provision of services to support this leisure travel.

The widely accepted definition of tourism is the one given by the International Union of Official Travel Organization (IUOTO), now the World Tourism Organization (WTO), in a UN conference on "International Travel and

Tourism" held in Rome in 1963. The definition is a refinement of an earlier definition given by the "Committee of the Statistical Experts of the League of Nations" in 1973. The term "visitor" described as "any person visiting a country other than in which he has his usual place of residence, for any reason other than following an occupation remunerated from within the country visited".The definition covers "Tourist", i. e., temporary visitors staying at least 24 hours in the country visited and the purpose of whose journey can be classified under one of the following headings: (i) leisure, (recreation, holiday, health, and sports), (ii) business, family, mission and meeting. For the term "temporary visitors", generally it is agreed to take the minimum duration of stay of 24 hours, where as the maximum extent is fixed at not more than 6 months (UN, 1963). The definition of tourism as given by Hunziker and Krapt, Swiss professors, has drawn considerable attention and has been accepted by the International Association of Scientific Experts on Tourism. They define it as "Tourism is the sum of phenomenon and relationship arising from the travel and stay of non-residents, in so far as they do not lead to permanent residence and are not connected with any earning activity". Tourism has become a popular global leisure activity. It is regarded by many countries, particularly resource-poor countries, as a potential stimulus to the economy. Yet tourism, by the nature of the activities involved, is constrained by the natural resource base and infrastructure, and by the pollution and other environmental and social impacts of tourist numbers (Brown et al. 1997).

Large volume international tourism is primarily a phenomenon of the last fifty years, and global mass tourism to developing countries, has developed on a large scale in the last few decades. At a global level, the number of tourist arrivals has risen from slightly over 25 million in the 1950s to 806 million in 2005, corresponding to an average annual growth rate of 6.5% (World Tourism Organization, 2006; Tadesse, 2009). The World Tourism Organization (WTO) reports that tourist activity in terms of numbers of visits has risen by 7% each year, with an increase of 12.5% in receipts, excluding international air fares. During the past decade, there has been an average growth rate of 4% despite the world recession. The WTO has also reported that global annual receipts increased of 9% between 1990 and 2000. During these years, Asia and Oceania are expected to gain a larger proportion of global tourist demand, from 14.7% in 1989 to 21.9% by 2000. The volume of tourists is still increasing, an increase which looks likely to continue over the next few decades (Hameed, 1999). This mass tourism is not without disadvantages. The impacts of tourism, on the environment and on local social, economic and cultural life, are often detrimental. This has been documented in a range of countries, both in the north and south, rich and poor nations.

Tourism is now considered one of the world's largest industry with in an annual outlay of over US$ 3.5 trillion output, i.e., 6% of world GDP and employs 212 million people (at tenth of the world's work force) (McLaren, 1993). This sector is remaining high on the international agenda of development. The 7th session of the commission *Sustainable Development* focused on tourism and subsequently work programmes on sustainable tourism are being developed. The UN declared 2002 as the International Year of Tourism and the World Tourism Organization adopted a Global Code of Ethics for tourism in its General Assembly held in Santiago de Chile, from September 27 until October 1, 1990. WTO forecasts that the arrivals will reach 1 billion in the year 2010 and that by 2020 it will reach 1.6 billion nearly three times the number of international trips made in 1996, which was 592 million (Groth, 2000; Maharana, 2000; Tadesse, 2009).

Tourism accounts for the higher share of world trade than cars, oil and is the main export for many small developing countries. Highly labour intensive, the sector provides vital employment for people with a wide range of skills as well as the un-skilled. Why is important to pay attention to tourism as a potential source of growth and development in poor countries? Firstly, it is a major industry. If we include related activities, tourism and general travel are 11% of world GDP. Exports of tourism services are about 6-7% in 1995 of total exports of goods and services. It rose from about 4% in 1980 to 5% in 1990 and 6% in 1995. Secondly, tourism is growing faster in developing world than elsewhere as the data from the World Tourism Organization (WTO) arrivals, receipts and receipts per visitor all grew faster in developing countries than elsewhere during the 1990's, and Thirdly, many of the countries in which tourism is important are among the poorest and least developed countries in the world. The growing significance of tourism to developing countries is:

(i) Since the 1950's developing countries have received increasing number of international tourists, mainly from developed countries. Developing countries had 292.6 million international arrivals in 2000, an increase since 1990 of nearly 95%. The sub group of least developed countries (LDCS) had 5.1 million international arrivals in 2000. They achieved an increase of nearly 75% in the decade. This performance by developing countries compares very favourably with the growth of tourism to countries of OECD and the EU, which achieved around 40% growth, (WTO, 2002).

(ii) Over the last ten years there has been a higher rate of growth in the absolute value of tourism expenditure as recorded in the national accounts in developing countries than in developed countries. The absolute earnings of developing countries grew by 133% between 1990 and 2000, and in the LDCS by 154% this compares with 64% of OECD countries and 49% for EU countries, (WTO, 2002).

(iii) The developing countries particularly LDCS secured a larger increase in the income per international arrival between1990 and 2000 than did the OECD or the EU. The LDCS secured an increase of 45% between 1990 and 2000 and the developing countries nearly 20%, this compares with 18% for OECD countries and 7.8% for the EU, (WTO, 2002).

(iv) In developing countries the export value of tourism grew by 154% (between 1990 and 2000) second only to the growth in the manufacturing sector (Tadesse, 2009).

Developing countries are relatively important in the international industry as a whole on the basis of the number of international visitors they receive, although only a few are major destinations. It is in some developing countries that tourism is growing fastest and /or making the largest contribution to the national economy. The importance of tourism to these economies shows that its effects go well beyond those countries that are important international destinations or are well known for their dependency.

Land-use and tourism has been recognized as one of the major drivers of global change in biodiversity over the past several decades (Rai and Sundriyal, 1997; Sala et al. 2000; Hansen et al. 2004). Over the same period, protected areas have expanded globally in order to conserve biological and cultural resources (Rodriguez and Young, 2000; Chape et al. 2003; Zimmerer et al. 2004). It is recognized that protected areas are effecting in protecting some kinds of native species still occur inside resources (Woodroffe and Cinsberg, 1998).

Mass tourism has recently inflicted adverse impact on environment of mountain areas (Pawson et al. 1984; Zuric, 1992; and Rai and Sundriyal, 1997). Budowski (1976) identified three different relationships between tourism and nature conservation: conflict, coexistence, and symbiosis. He noted that unplanned or poorly-planned tourism in areas of conservation significance can often lead to conflict. He also pointed out that there were examples which prove that a change of attitude leading to a symbiotic relationship between tourism and conservation can lead to physical, cultural, ethical and economic benefits to a country (Kenchington, 1989).

Nature-based tourism denotes all tourism directly dependent on the use of natural resources in a relatively undeveloped state, including scenery, topography, water features, vegetation and wildlife etc., thus it includes hunting, countryside motor biking and white-water rafting, even if the use of the natural resources by the tourist is neither wise nor sustainable (Butler, 1992; Ceballos-Lascurain, 1996). There has been a growing interest over the past two decades on ecotourism with emphasis in conservation of biodiversity and cultural heritage, which attract a majority of tourists. The goal of "ecotourism" is to capture a portion of the enormous global tourism market by attracting visitors to natural areas and using the revenues to fund local conservation and full economic development (Ziffer, 1989). Protected areas of biodiversity interest provide a variety of benefits and services, which are essential for the economic development of a region. National parks have become tourist icons with many countries promoting some of their parks as "must-see attractions". In some cases the attraction to visit individual parks is as much a product of marketing as it is of accessibility. In other cases, the uniqueness of places is often the sole reason why tourists visit them (Boyd, et al. 1994).

Historically, the increase of nature-based and ecotourism worldwide was largely a result of the increase in awareness of the plight of the World's dwindling biological diversity and a reaction against mass tourism and its demonstrative effort of conservation issues. The conservation of biological diversity, usually shortened to biodiversity, is now seen as a priority of national governments and the general community. In conceptual terms, the linkages between local tourism participation and conservation have not been properly discussed in the ecotourism literature. Therefore, the primary goal of this book is to create a shared knowledge about people and natural resources in developing countries with a focus on the National Park and its surrounding area. The aim is to analyses trends, present need and options in relation to point of view and synthesis knowledge and opportunities for sustainable development. It also aims to give correct recommendation about how to priorities and plan multi-sectoral development activities. Finally, it will serve as a basis for monitoring and impact assessment accompanying a local and induced development.

1.2. THE CONCEPT OF TOURIST AREA EVOLUTION

There can be little doubt that tourist areas are dynamic, that they evolve and change over time. This evolution is brought about by a variety of factors including changes in the preferences and needs of visitors, the gradual deterioration and possible replacement of physical plant and facilities, and the change (or even disappearance) of the original natural and cultural attractions which were responsible for the initial popularity of the area. In some cases, while these attractions remain, they may be utilized for different purposes or come to be regarded as less significant in comparison with imported attractions (Wolfe, 1952).

Plog (1972) suggested that tourist areas are attractive to different types of visitors as the areas evolve, beginning with small numbers of adventuresome allocentrics, followed by increasing numbers of mid centrics as the area becomes accessible, better serviced, and well known, and giving way to declining numbers of psychocentrics as the area becomes older, more outdated, and less different to the areas of origin of visitors. While the actual numbers of visitors may not decline for a long time, the potential market will reduce in size as the area has to compete with others that are more recently developed. Noronha (1976) has suggested that "Tourism develops in three stages: (i) discovery; (ii) local response and initiative; and (iii) institutionalized. It is also explicit in Christaller's concept that types of tourists change with the tourist areas.

Visitors will come to an area in small numbers initially, restricted by lack of access, facilities, and local knowledge. As facilities are provided and awareness grows, number of visitors will increase. With marketing, information dissemination, and further facility provision, the area's popularity will grow rapidly. Eventually, however, the rate of increase in visitor numbers will decline as levels of carrying capacity are reached. These may be identified in terms of environmental factors (e.g. land scarcity, water quality, air quality), of physical plant (e.g. transportation, accommodation, other services), or of social factors (e.g. crowding, resentment by the local population). As the attractiveness of the area declines relative to other areas, because of overuse and the impacts of visitors, the actual number of visitors may also eventually decline (Butler, 1980). In a few localities, limits to the growth of tourism have been adopted, chiefly because of severe environmental damage to attractions.

1.3. TOURISM VERSUS ECOTOURISM

For developing countries, a rapidly growing tourism industry has proved to be an increasingly important source of foreign exchange inflows. Nature tourism, a particularly dynamic sub-sector, is an important tool for generating employment and income in underdeveloped, biodiversity rich Third World regions because it requires comparatively small investments. Conservationists also look to nature tourism as a potential "win-win" strategy of sustainable development, where tourist spending constitutes a much-needed instrument for capitalizing on biodiversity and natural sites (Wunder, 2000).

Over the last three decades, there has been growing debate on the magnitude of tourism in developing countries, and its impacts and implications in the host regions are enormous. Due to tremendous growth and its adverse consequences in the host region, the concept of tourism has now changed from mass tourism to ecotourism/responsible tourism/nature oriented tourism. Ecotourism is currently a "hot topic". The concept of ecotourism is now gaining overwhelming response in the recent years. Ecotourism is an exciting new venture, which combines the pleasures of discovering spectacular flora and fauna, and understanding their values with an opportunity to contribute to their protection. The greening of tourism is essential for the ecological and sociological advancement and sustainability of the industry. For ecotourism to be a tool for conservation and economic development, several groups must participate at all stages in its evolution. Officials from the national tourism bureau, park service, NGOs and finance department are all part of ecotourism development. They are the ones responsible for putting the policies and structures in place that will enable its successful development. Communities surrounding protected areas are generally overlooked in ecotourism development and management. Localcommunities are often dependent on the natural resources that attract tourists. If communities are not involved and do not receive some benefit, they may compete with the industry for use of the natural resources.

Ecotourism is a new idea that has captured the attention of many people. Protected area managers are facing increasing numbers of visitors to parks and reserves. Residents living near protected areas are seeing more tourists and trying to decide whether they want to get involved and how to maintain control over their homelands. Rural development specialists are investigating ecotourism's economic potential. Sociologists are studying whether there is anything valuable for native communities in this net work. Conservationists want to determine if ecotourism is a legitimate tool for preserving biological diversity and promoting sustainable development. Government officials are considering ecotourism as a new source of foreign exchange. Private sector funding agencies are evaluating the financial viability of ecotourism investments. Travelers are visiting parks and reserves worldwide like never before and are looking to these experiences as a way to understand and appreciate the natural environment (Boo, 1992).

Nature-based tourism and recreation, including in protected areas is increasing worldwide. In the global tourism industry, nature tourism is becoming increasingly popular in terms of numbers of visitors. Ecotourism seems to be a catch-all word that means many things to many people. To some it means ecologically sound tourism. To others it is synonymous with nature tourism. A number of terms are used to describe such travel, with nature tourism and ecotourism being most widely used. One category of term is merely descriptive. The expressions nature-travel, adventure-travel, and cultural-travel segment tourists based on what activities they participate during their visit. Another category of terms are value-based. The phrases, responsible tourism, alternative tourism, and ethical travel, highlight the need for considering the approach and impact of travel regardless of the activities pursued. Ceballos-Lascurain (1988) eloquently combines these two aspects, the activity and the approach, in his definition of ecotourism (Box 2).

Box 2.

"Tourism that involves traveling to relatively undisturbed or uncontaminated natural areas with specific object of studying, admiring, and enjoying the scenery and its wild plants and animals, as well as any existing cultural aspects (both past and present) found in these areas. Ecological tourism implies a scientific, aesthetic or philosophical approach, although the ecological tourist is not required to be a professional scientist, artist or philosopher. The main point is that the person who practices ecotourism has the opportunity of immersing him or herself in nature in a way most people cannot enjoy in their routine, urban existences. This person will eventually acquire a consciousness that will convert him into somebody keenly involved in conservation issues".

Nature tourism consists of travel to a particular natural site largely for amenity and recreational purposes, and is, as we have said, a rapidly growing sub-component of global tourism. *Ecotourism* is distinguished from nature tourism as it includes some aspects of conservation or enhancement of the environment, a strong commitment to nature and a sense of social responsibility. Ecotourism, the fastest growing sector of the largest industry on the earth, is strongly advocated by major conservation groups as a way to help conserve nature (Taylor et al. 2003). It's potential for generating income while creating incentives for conservation has sparked academic discussion regarding the meaning of ecotourism and attention to the design of integrated conservation and tourism projects (Gossling, 1999; Wunder, 2000). Ecotourism is nature travel that advances conservation and sustainable development efforts.

Even though a standardized definition of ecotourism does not yet exist (IUCN, 1993; Hvenegaard, 1994), most experts suggest ecotourism should achieve specific conservation and development goals (Boo, 1990; Buckley, 1994; Lindberg et al. 1996; Wallace and Pierce, 1996). The World Conservation Union (IUCN) and the Ecotourism Society define ecotourism as "responsible travel to natural areas that conserves the environment and sustains the well-being of local people" (Lindberg and Hawkins, 1993). Definitions focus on 'environmentally responsible' tourism (Ceballos-Lascurain, 1993) that provides 'direct benefits' to the nature conservation area and to 'the economic welfare of local residents' (Ziffer, 1989), or a 'nature tourism that promotes conservation and sustainable development' (Boo, 1990). This implies that some attempts are made to balance the needs of tourism, conservation and culture, that it is more pro-active in terms of not only stemming negative impacts to the environment, but also in some way trying to enhance the local environment. The criteria for ecotourism employed in the literature may be summarized as follows: (i) minimal physical and social impacts on the visited area; (ii) ecological education of the tourist at the natural site; and (iii) notable economic participation by local residents.

There are many other definitions sprinkled throughout the literature and an academic circle which has thrived on the analysis of the "ecotourism" phenomenon. In the tourism industry as a whole the terms "ecotourism" and "nature-based tourism" are almost always used interchangeably and indiscriminately. There will never be a firm division between tourism and ecotourism. Ecotourists must define themselves as an avant-garde camp that brings out the best of the tourism market and provides a model for the rest of the world (Wood, 1992).

Rather than suggesting that nature-based or ecotourism is a separate sector of the industry, the Ecologically Sustainable Development Working Group on Tourism (ESDWG, 1991) suggested that *Ecotourism* is a situation where 'the idea of symbiotic relationship between tourism and environment" becomes most apparent and that tourism facilities and services exist in a continuum, from those which are natural resource dependent for their operation, through those which are independent of natural resources. Ecotourism and Nature-based can form part of many types of travelers' experiences, varying from a few hours of nature-appreciation, through to intensive long-duration tours of a month or more.

The benefits and costs of ecotourism can be seen from many perspectives. The primary benefits of ecotourism are: (i) increased funding for protected areas and local communities; (ii) new jobs created for local residents; and (iii) environmental education for visitors. Of greater significance, ecotourism presents opportunities to advance conservation and development goals. It offers ways to capture more attention and funds for conservation and development efforts (Boo, 1992).

There are three primary factors influencing the level of ecotourism demand i.e., overall tourism growth, the growth in specialty travel, and increasing awareness and concern for the environment. Overall tourism, for example, is expected to grow by about 45% per year for next ten years because of macro factors such as population growth, rising world incomes and employment, shorter work weeks in many parts of the world, and the increasing globalization of the world's economies and societies. Finally, cultural dynamics also leave their mark as evidenced by the change in attitudes about vacation time amongst professionals (Ziffer, 1989). On the supply side of travel, many traditional destinations have reached a saturation point and tour operators have packaged exotic locals to peddle to consumers looking for an escape from the throngs.

Nevertheless, nature-based tourism is a rapidly growing sector of the tourism economy. Its global value for 1988 has been estimated to be as high as US$ 1 trillion (Filion, et al. 1992). So, it has often proved to be a powerful incentive for conservation in many parts of the world. Tourism is one of the prime sectors that can support more people, if carefully planned and well worked economic "Niche" are created (Sreedhar, 1995). The UNCED'S agenda 21, chapter 13 identified tourism as one of the key activities to provide alternative livelihood opportunities to mountain people in the process of attaining sustainable mountain development (Keating, 1993). WTO (1999) has been given priorities to community involvement in tourism, with local communities participating in the tourism planning and development process of their area through participation. Ecotourism is reliant on natural phenomena in relatively undisturbed sites (Boyed et al. 1994), such as protected areas. Before being promoted, the impacts of ecotourism must be thoroughly examined in the context of a protected area's mandate.

For ecotourism to be a tool for conservation and economic development, several groups viz., government officials, protected area personnel, local communities, tourism industry, NGOs, financial institutions and consumers must participate at all stages in its evaluation.

1.4. BIODIVERSITY: DEFINITION, SIGNIFICANCE AND VALUATION

Biodiversity or biological diversity which simply stated as the variety and variability of all animals, plants and micro-organisms on earth (Reid and Miller, 1989; Bridgewater et al. 1992; and Flint, 1992). It is the "blanket" term for the full complement of the natural biological wealth, with the breadth of the concept reflected in the interrelatedness of genes, species and ecosystems. Throughout the world, the loss of biodiversity through the extinction of species, the conversion and degradation of natural habitats, and the disruption of ecological processes is occurring at an unprecedented rate (Pearce and Moran, 1994). Biological diversity is a public good, and species and ecosystems in one part of the world can provide significant benefits to distant nations. Much of the depletion of biological diversity over the past 400 years or so has been caused by powerful global forces, countries (McNeely, 1988).

Biodiversity conservation is a relatively recent term which embraces and springs from the concepts of conservation of national parks and wilderness, wildlife, landscapes and ecosystems, and is the result of better understanding of the needs for conservation of biological diversity. Biodiversity can be considered in terms of genes, species and ecosystems. Frequently, biodiversity is thought as simply the variety of animals and plants, partly because they are the most conspicuous elements of biodiversity. The genetic variety, that is the variety within a species, is equally important, as is the variety of ecosystems, or the way in which the plants, animals and micro-organisms organize themselves in relation to each other and the biotic or non-living world. Species diversity is the variety of living organisms on the earth, and ecosystem diversity relates to the variety of habitats, biotic communities and ecological processes in the biosphere.

The concept of national park is only one type of area protection, alongside world heritage sites, wilderness areas, biosphere reserves, marine reserves and nature reserves. The national park and world heritage labels have become important in tourism promotion, and they are frequently seen in marketing (Plamer, 1999). Eagles (2001) suggests that the names national park and world heritage site have a significant brand identity and thus are more attractive than less-known names like "conservation area". Nolte (2004) concludes from her study about tourism in biosphere reserves, that national parks and world heritage sites are well known labels to many people and that they have a strong brand mark, as compared to biosphere reserve, which is hardly noticed. According to Eagles (2001), the name national park is closely associated with nature-based tourism, and is a symbol of high quality natural environment with well-designed infrastructure. Designation may suggest that the area is pristine, with recreational opportunities undisturbed by risk of encounter with motor vehicles, for example, and that the area is managed to provide solitude (Loomis, 1998). Earlier studies have discussed the importance of protected areas and labels in tourism, and that area protection can be an important marker, but the extent to which designations in fact influence actual visitation have not been extensively empirically examined.

India's biodiversity is mostly contained in its vast common property resources, viz. forests, wetlands, coastal and marine areas, grasslands and other habitats that are under the control of government agencies or village bodies. For the past few decades, legal and administrative protection to these ecosystems and to notified animal and plant species has been the main strategy for biodiversity conservation in India. The declaration of national parks, sanctuaries and other categories of protected areas under the Wildlife (Protection) Act, 1972, have resulted in protecting a large number of areas from certain destruction by commercial, industrial or biotic forces. Protected areas extend to around 5% of the geographical area of India, and consist of both national parks and sanctuaries. It was observed that 56% of the national parks and 72% of the sanctuaries had settlements of human population within the protected area and 83% of the parks and 87% of the sanctuaries had a population adjacent to the protected area. About 43% of the parks and 68% of the sanctuaries accorded and accepted rights of local communities such as to grazing by livestock, harvesting of timber and collection of minor forest produce (Chopra, 2002).

1.4.1. Valuation: Concept and Levels

Since past two decades, the estimation of economic values of cultural goods and service has drawn the attention of economists (Navrud and Ready, 2002; Noonan, 2003 and Venkatachalam, 2004 cited in Choi et al. 2010; Kaminski et al. 2007). Alternative concepts of value relevant for different kinds of resources are available in the literature. In order to compete for the attention of government decision-makers, conservation policies first need to demonstrate in economic terms the value of biological diversity to the country's social and economic development. Typically in valuation studies the interest is in estimating total economic value, which includes not only use values (for example, activities and services), but also intangible non-use values (for example, educational, bequest and altruistic values) not normally captured in private market transactions. Total economic value can be estimated using stated preference non-market valuation techniques (Bateman et al. 2002 and Noonan, 2003), such as CVM and CM.

There is a need to discuss with some clarifications concerning terminology used in environmental economics. *Use* and *Non-use* values are often used to delineate different types of goods and services provided by natural resources. Varying definitions have been proposed by economists. In this I choose to follow the delineation formulated by Freeman (1993) which defines "natural resources value that are independent of people's present use of the resource" as non-use values. Consequently, use values can then been defined as those benefits attributed to immediate present consumption of resource. Approaches for determining the value of biological resources include (McNeely, 1988):

a) Direct values

    (i)   Consumptive use value: This is the value placed on nature's products that are consumed directly, without passing through a market. When direct consumption involves recreation, as in sport, fishing and hunting, most economists estimate consumptive use value as the value of the whole recreational experience.

    (ii)   Productive use value: This value is assigned to products which are commercially harvested, and is, therefore, often the only value of biological resources which is reflected in national income accounts. Estimates of such values are usually made at the production end (landed value, harvest value, farm gate value etc.) rather than at the retail end, where values are much higher.

b) Indirect values

    (i)   Non consumptive use value: Environmental resources generally speaking, nature's functions or services rather than goods provide value without being consumed, traded in the market-place, or reflected in national income accounts. A non-consumptive use such as organized tourism based on biological resources (such as visits to a national park) can often provide a powerful economic justification for conserving biological resources, particularly when protected areas are a primary attraction for visitors to a country.

    (ii)   Option value: Option value is a means of assigning a value to risk aversion in the face of uncertainty.

    (iii)   Existence value: Value attached to the ethical feelings of existence, which reflects the sympathy, responsibility and concern that some people may feel toward species and ecosystems.

In the case of environmental goods and services, observed market behaviour is not always an option. In such cases, economists may use surrogate market activities to act as a reflection of the value of the amenity. Freeman (1993) cites four different techniques within this category: travel cost method, hedonic property values, avoidance expenditures and referendum voting. The travel cost method has been widely used in developed countries because of its appealing use of observed consumer behaviour. Hedonic property values are estimates of amenity values from environmental resources which can be observed by increases in property values (Portney, 1981). Avoidance expenditures provide a third method for indirectly estimating the value of environmental goods. Generally, this method is used for cases such as air or water pollution. This method is not useful for valuing protected areas. Referendum voting method uses estimates the value of an environmental amenity implicit in the demonstrated willingness to pay of voters based upon special referendum issues.

.   However, when reliable market data are not available researchers may need to create a hypothetical market to elicit consumer preferences. For example, cultural institutions and heritage sites often provide a variety of public contributions such as symbolic cultural items, historical value, social value, aesthetic value, spiritual value, educational value and shared experience (Hansen et al. 1998; Sable and Kling, 2001 and Throsby, 2001). These are public goods, and their economic values are not easily determined from transactions in actual markets.

In stated preference methods, respondents are asked to directly state how much they are willing to pay (or accept) for the given good (through CVM). The most common form of hypothetical method for evaluating environmental goods and services is the contingent valuation method (CVM), which asks respondents to place a monetary value on the described environmental good. Typically, the contingent valuation method provides background on the environmental good, and, then, using various survey designs, elicits a monetary value of the good from the respondent. The major advantage of contingent valuation studies is their adaptability for different environmental amenities (Murthy and Menkhaus, 1994).

Contingent valuation, however, has been heavily criticized for its subjective nature. One of the most important critiques, as is often the case with social science research, is that the surveys are subject to a number of biases. Strategic bias may occur if respondents deliberately overstate or understate the value of a good in order to manipulate policy decisions in their favour. An information bias may occur if the respondents are not given complete information regarding the hypothetical scenario. Instrument bias occurs when the method of payment in the hypothetical situation causes the respondents to alter bias can be demonstrated by the different responses which could result when people are offered the option of donating money to a cause versus having higher taxes, and finally, as with any survey in the social sciences, the sampling bias, or non-respondent case of an externality. Typically a contingent valuation method is designed to assess the economic impact of a quantitative or qualitative change in the good or service provided.

1.5. Relationship between Biodiversity and Nature Based Tourism

Ecotourism can capture biodiversity values and provide incentives for conservation, and many integrated conservation and development projects including ecotourism component. One key assumption behind this strategy is that ecotourism businesses can achieve financial viability (OHL-Schacherer et al. 2008). Ecotourism was a natural reaction to mainstream tourism, which was perceived to be the major contributor to the degradation of the natural attraction on which it is based (Box 3). Yet from the point of view of conservation of biodiversity, it does not matter at all whether visitors to an area are led by a trained or untrained guide, or whether the tour is classified as an eco-tour or a large group day trip. Himalayan biodiversity, one of the main resources of tourism, is under severe threat, with many ecosystems and species are suffering serious declines (personal observation).

The need for environmental protection and rehabilitation was also recognized by the government and local people, which found that "a major motivation for tourism activities in Himalayan region, both domestic and international, is to experience aspects of Himalayan natural and cultural environment. Tourism development which exploits and degrades the environment is not only contrary to the principle of Biodiversity Convention, but is also likely to be ultimately self-defeating". In a positive light, the relationship between biodiversity and nature based ecotourism can and should be mutually reinforcing. On the one hand, the declared and the publicly promoted protection of natural features, ecosystems and biodiversity acts as a strong attractor for the tourism trade and provide a vehicle for the development of national and regional economies. On the other hand, there are opportunities and indeed a strong obligation for the tourism trade to promote and contribute to biodiversity conservation.

Box 3. Ecotourism and Biodiversity Conservation (Christ et al. 2003)

Ecotourism can directly contribute to biodiversity conservation by:
• Offering less destructive livelihood alternatives to local communities and landowners in buffer zones and conservation corridors, away from unregulated logging, intensive cattle-ranching, monoculture, hunting and unsustainable tourism;
• Providing an incentive for public and private landowners in critical ecosystems to permanently conserve biodiversity-rich properties, by offering revenue-producing, low impact economic use;
• Providing protected area managers with additional financial resources from visitation and donations; and
• Raising visitor's awareness, promoting community involvement and interest in conservation issues and generating political support for conservation through environmental education during travel.

The Hindu-Kush Himalayan region is a unique area in the world offering rich biodiversity, culture, socio-economic traditions, history and lifestyles. From times immemorial lofty mountain ranges, rich resources of natural environments and biodiversity are valuable economic assets for tourism and have attracted tourists, pilgrims, naturalists, explorers, trekkers, mountaineers and other various adventure travelers. For the tourist, biodiversity conservation is most obvious at the ecosystem or species level in areas of natural beauty and ecological interest, such as the Khangchendzonga Biosphere Reserves. Tourism is recognized as a major user of biological resources while also providing employment for many people (Rai and Sundriyal, 1997). Numerous opportunities and benefits can be derived by strategically integrating biodiversity conservation requirements with future tourism needs. Ziffer (1989), for example, has suggested that "the goal of ecotourism is to capture a portion of the enormous global tourism market by attracting visitors to natural areas and using the revenues to fund local conservation and fuel economic development.

1.6. TOURISM: NATIONAL INCOME AND REGIONAL DEVELOPMENT

Tourism, as a major source of foreign exchange, plays an important role in the balance of payments and overall developments of a country. As a matter of fact, "tourism represents the most effective manner of transforming resources from the affluent to the developing societies" (Kayastha, 1973). It is second

largest money spinner in the world and is likely to out strip even oil in the near
future (Singh, 1986). Tourism brings a substantial increase in the GNP and in
employment. The foreign tourism balance is calculated by subtracting the money
spent by the nationals abroad from the total foreign exchange received from the
tourists. When all the leakages, which are mainly through the purchase of foreign
goods and expenditures on promotion and publicity abroad, are deducted from the
foreign exchange received by the tourists, the net foreign exchange tourism
income is obtained (Lawson and Baud-Bovy, 1977).

1.6.1. Tourism Multiplier

The money spent by a tourist circulates through the economy and stimulates
it, as it frequently changes hands and is spent a number of times. This creates a
chain reaction in the economy. The value of tourism multiplier varies from nation
to nation depending upon the state of economy. The formula for estimating the
tourism multiplier (k) is as follows (Bryden and Faber, 1971):

K= 1 / (m.p.s + m.p.i)

Where: m.p.s- stands for "marginal propensity to save", and m.p.i- stands for
"marginal propensity to import or to spend".

1.6.2. Local Community and Tourism

Tourism is affecting the lives of rural people across the world. For some
communities, it is a driving force of development, for others it brings mainly
negative impacts. In most communities, the impacts are highly differentiated. In
either case, the type of involvement people have helps shape the benefits and costs
they experience as a result.

Nature-based tourism and tourism to developing countries are among the
fastest growing sectors of the tourism industry, (Wells, 1992; Ceballos-Lascuarin,
1996) which is itself the world's largest and fastest-growing industry. Tourism
currently generates 10% of world income, and employs ten percent of the world's
workforce. It is expected to have doubled in size by the year 2015, with an
anticipated one billion tourists per year, of which, 25% of are expected to be
visiting a developing country (Newbery, 1998). These statistics mean that tourism
has enormous potential to influence development in rural communities where

much nature tourism occurs, and where the search for ever-more exotic destinations continues.

To date, tourism has generated significant benefits for some developing countries, becoming an economic mainstay, and significant source of foreign exchange and employment. For example, in many of the Caribbean islands, tourism has overtaken agriculture as the major contributor to GDP. It has brought economic development to remote areas with little comparative advantage in other industries. However, in several places the economic benefits have been minimized through 'leakage' while tourism has also led to displacement of local people to make way for tourist developments, depletion of local water supplies, over-burdening of local infrastructure etc. Enhancing their active *involvement* in the industry is essential if the potential benefits of tourism are to be maximized and the negatives to be minimized.

The *tourism industry* is recognizing the need to work with local people because of their central role in maintaining cultural and natural heritage, which are of interest to tourists. Some operators are focusing on involvement of local people as an element of 'ecotourism,' in response to market trends which now emphasize that tourism should be socially as well as environmentally responsible. The 'ecotourism' label can, however, be used simply as a marketing gimmick. These may include local employment in tourism industries; enterprises run by local entrepreneurs or communities; self-employment; making partnership agreements with tourism operators; and local residents participating in local planning of tourism, wildlife, parks, and related land-uses.

1.7. POLICY DIRECTIONS

There are many different ways in which government influences the form of tourism and the opportunities for community involvement or benefit. Internationally, the broad objective of integrating development with the protection of species and ecosystem was emphasized by the World Commission of Environment and Development (1987). In a significant step forward in international environment law, the International Convention on Biological Diversity, which came into force internationally on 29 December 1993, and to which India is a party, explicitly integrate the conservation and sustainable use of biodiversity. Other important measures in the convention are the enhancement of knowledge and understanding of biological diversity and the impacts on it. Parties are required to identify and monitor important ecosystems, species and genetic components of biological diversity as well as processes and activities that have or likely to have significant adverse impacts on biological diversity. In this way, countries are able to determine the priorities with regard to conservation and sustainable use measures, which need to be undertaken. Integration of biodiversity conservation and tourism development has emerged as an important national objective, with strong support by government, industry and the community.

Parties are required to give emphasis to in-situ conservation through a broad range of actions, including the establishment and management of protected areas; conservation and sustainable use of biological resources within and outside protected areas; promotion of environmentally sound and sustainable development in areas adjacent to protected areas; rehabilitation and restoration of degraded ecosystems; control of alien species and genetically modified organisms; protection of threatened species and populations; and regulation of damaging processes and activities (Ashley and Roe, 1998).

The tourism policy of the Government of India was announced in November, 1982. It helps bring socio-economic benefits to the community and the state in terms of employment opportunities, income generation, revenue generation for the states, foreign exchange earnings and in general causes habitat improvement. The Planning Commission's suggestion that Tourism should be declared an industry appears to be a precursor to the policy perspective. The Seventh Plan (1985-90) advocated a two-pronged thrust in area of development of tourism, viz, to vigorously promote domestic tourism and to diversify overseas tourism in India.

A national Committee on Tourism was set up in July, 1986 by the Planning Commission to prepare a perspective plan for the sector. However, by September, 1987, the Central Government declared more concessions for the sector, i.e., tax exemption on foreign exchange earnings from tourism. The Tourism Development Finance Corporation was also set up in 1987 with a corpus fund of Rs.100 crores. The eighth Plan document made a special mention that the future expansion of tourism should be achieved mainly by private sector participation. The thrust areas include development of selected tourist places, diversification from cultural related tourism to holiday and leisure tourism, development of trekking, winter sports, wildlife, exploring new source markets particularly to lure high spending tourists, restoration of national heritage projects, providing inexpensive accommodation in different tourist centers etc.

For the first time in Sikkim, government initiated a common platform for a private and public sector dialogue on tourism and biodiversity conservation. The sectoral approach of different departments was inadequate in addressing the management aspect in a holistic manner. The various private sector stakeholders who were engaged in tourism operation had their own problems and expected incentives from the government. The two prime stakeholder groups were involved since April 1995. The local community, which is an integral component of ecotourism development, had a limited approach with the government, but this was significantly strengthened in few years. In due course of time the local community-based conservation group has been empowered by various agencies to monitor and implement conservation activities. Workshops and meetings have increased the level of public and private sector interactions and awareness of tourism and conservation-related issues. A central element of the existing policy is that all foreign visitors need an entry permit to visit Sikkim for a maximum duration of 15 days. Travel agencies/Tour operators arrange trail routes and charge daily rates, including food and guides to the Khangchendzonga Biosphere Reserve.

As part of an approach to biodiversity conservation, ecotourism defined as environmentally and socially responsible tourism, clearly has a role to play in Hindu-Kush Himalayan region. As the number of visitors both domestic and international sectors increase, the need to be proactive on promoting and supporting a responsible tourism ethic among consumers, suppliers and producers alike is imperative. The most important feature of the enterprise-based approach was to provide a framework in which to analyze and develop the potential of tourism for more than one type of stakeholder. Furthermore, it provided a means to argue that long-term benefits from tourism would only be possible if those whose income depended on the activity had a greater decision-making power in natural resource management.

Chapter 2

BIODIVERSITY STATUS AND SIGNIFICANCE

2.1. INTRODUCTION

Biological diversity or biodiversity, a term that first emerged some twenty years ago (Lovejoy, 1980 a & b; Wilson, 1984; Norse et al. 1986; Wilson and Peters, 1988; Reid and Miller, 1989; McNeely et al. 1990), describes the variety and variability of life on earth. It encompasses all forms of terrestrial and aquatic plants, animals and micro-organisms, their genetic material and the ecosystem of which they are part. Biodiversity is not uniformly distributed on the earth, and could comprise 5 to more than 50 million species. Biodiversity is usually divided into three categories: genetic diversity, species diversity and ecosystem diversity (Box 1).

Box 1.

• Genetic diversityrefers to the differences in genetic make-up between distinct species and to generic variations within species.
• Species diversityrefers to the variety of species within a region.
• Ecosystem diversityis the variety of habitats, biotic communities, and ecological processes, as well as the diversity present within ecosystems.

Biodiversity is important to human being for their sustenance, health, well-being and recreation. The benefits of biodiversity conservation can be grouped into three broad categories: ecosystem services (conservation of water resources, soil conservation, nutrient storage and cycling, maintenance of ecosystems etc.), biological resources (food, medicines, forest products, population reservoirs, and future resources) and social benefits (research and education, recreation, cultural, and religious values). Systematic work on identifying and naming species has been in progress for the last 250 years. But still we have collected, described and named far less number of species than the actual number present (Singh et al. 2006).

The distribution and dynamics of biological resources must be understood to provide a rational basis for planning and management decisions, without which conservation of these resources in the natural habitat would be impossible (Khoshoo, 1992). Disturbance has become a widespread feature in most of the forests all over Himalaya (Singh and Singh, 1992), therefore, knowledge on ecological processes and biotic pressure can help in understanding the persistence of long-lived plant communities (Sundriyal and Sharma, 1996). Information on forest composition and association, biotic pressure and type of species surviving, and the extent of biomass removal can help to rejuvenate depleting forest through silvicultural practices and community involvement (Singh and Singh, 1987; Sunderiyal et al. 1994).

Biodiversity data and information are necessary to support well-informed decision making at the global to local level, yet information critical to such decisions is not available readily. Part of the problem is associated with the complex nature of biodiversity data and information given the uncertainties in terms of their existence and distribution. In addition, biodiversity data are scattered, outdated and available in incompatible formats and resolutions. There has been a lack of use of scientific information in the management programmes all over world but it is expected that in due course of time the outcome of scientific studies will be translated into management programmes (Sundriyal and Sharma, 1996).

The continued loss of biodiversity along with the reporting requirement of international conventions such as the Convention on Biological Diversity (CBD), Ramsar Convention, World Heritage Convention, etc. have called for extra efforts to generate better data and information. Moreover, baseline information on the status and distribution of biodiversity resources is necessary that can serve as a benchmark for monitoring. The purpose of this chapter is to examine the biodiversity status in the Himalaya in general and at the Khangchendzonga Biosphere Reserve especially in trekking corridor.

2.2. BIODIVERSITY: GLOBAL SIGNIFICANCE

Systematic work on identifying and naming species has been in progress for the last 250 years. The known and described number of species of all organisms on the earth is between 1.7 and 1.8 million, which is fewer than 15% of the actual number (Singh et al. 2006). The predicted number of total species varies from 5 to 30 million (Gaston, 1998) and average at 14 million. Only 4650 species of mammals are known to science. A large number of plant species (2, 70, 000) and vertebrates are known (Gibbs, 2001).

The accumulation of biodiversity on earth reflects the difference between the rates speciation and extinction. The overall natural extinction rate estimated from fossil data was 10^{-7} species per species per year (Ehrlich and Wilson, 1991). The global accumulation of biodiversity has occurred due to a range of evolutionary processes through time. According to Knoll (1984), there were about 25,000 flowering plant species some 125 million years ago, this number increased to 100,000 by the late Cretaceous and today there are more than 200,000 flowering plant species. The taxonomic richness of vascular plants through time indicates the following trends: a gradual increase between mid-Carboniferous and end-Permian, a minor reduction at the end of Permian, a rapid rebound to pre-Mesozoic level, a slow increase up to early-Cretaceous, previously dominant groups were replaced by Coniferophytes, Cycads, Cycadeoids, which dominated the plant biota until the mid-Cretaceous, the Angiosperms appeared in mid-Cretaceous and rapidly diversified in the Cenozoic (Signor, 1990).

Biodiversity is a source of economical wealth for many areas, such as many parks and forests, where wild nature and animals are a source of beauty and joy, attract many visitors. Ecotourism in particular, is a growing outdoor recreational activity. Biodiversity has also great aesthetic value. Examples of aesthetic rewards include ecotourism, bird watching, wildlife, pet keeping, gardening etc. Throughout human history, people have related biodiversity to the very existence of human race through cultural and religious beliefs. Today, we continue to recognize plants and animals as symbols of national pride and cultural heritage.

Biodiversity is not uniformly distributed across the geographical regions. Certain regions of the world are megadiversity zones. The IUCN Plant Conservation Office has identified 234 areas of especially high plant diversity around the world. These are located in north-western South America, Central America, Tropical Africa, Eastern Mediterranean region and South-east Asia, Malaysia.

2.2.1. Himalayan Significance

The rich biological treasures of the Himalaya may be their most precious natural resource, for they constitute a unique world of plant and animal species and contribute greatly to the genetic resources of the entire planet. Detailed biological surveys indicate that the mountains constitute one of the planet's great biodiversity centers. The high percentage of native endangered species located in the eastern section of the range makes it one of the planet's top twenty "biodiversity hotspots" (Box 2) of the Indian sub-continent that harbors the largest number of endemics and endangered species (Khoshoo, 1992). This region comprises of parts of the eastern Nepal, Bhutan, China, Chittagaon (Bangladesh) and north-eastern states of India including hills of Darjeeling. It forms a meeting ground of Indo-Malayan and Indo-Chinese bio-geographical realms as well as Himalayan and Peninsular Indian elements that has given rise to a very rich biodiversity. Based on the survey about 65% area of the total geographical area of the country as many as 46000 plant species and 81,000 animal species have been reported from India (Rai, 1998). This rich biodiversity is continuing genetic elements evolved over basis of life and contain millions of years.

Box 2.

> Myers introduced the term hot spots in 1988 for the geographical regions particularly rich in endemic, rare and threatened species found in relatively small areas but facing significant threats of habitat loss. The 34 hot spots now contain about 75% of the world's most threatened mammals, birds, and amphibians and about 50% of all plants and 42% of land vertebrates (Conservation International, 2005, Ebert, 2005).

In the Eastern Himalaya, Sikkim (total area 9253 km^2 that includes 7096 km^2 of Sikkim and 2157 km^2 of Darjeeling) spreads over Sikkim and the hill regions of Darjeeling that harbors more than 26% of the flowering plants of India and is an important phyto-geographic reserve of the country. This region is listed among the world's ten most critical centers for biodiversity and endemism with 150 species of mammals, 550 species of birds, 650 species of butterflies and moths, 33 species of reptiles, 16 species of amphibians, 48 species of fishes, 4500 species of flowering plants, 36 species of rhododendrons, 9 species of conifers, 430 species of orchids, 350 species of ferns and allies, and 175 species of wild edible plants (Pradhan, 1976, 1979; Pradhan and Lachungpa, 1990; Tamang, 1993; Rai and

Rai, 1993; Sundriyal and Sharma, 1996, Singh and Chauhan, 1998; Lachungpa, 1998; Sundriyal, 1999).

This region supports luxuriant tropical, temperate and alpine vegetation in its most pristine and virgin form. Sikkim is a centre of biodiversity, due to the variety of landscapes and climatic conditions, which range from tropical to alpine. An analysis of dominant families of flowering plants clearly indicates the floristic richness of this state (Table 2.1). The alpine areas are known worldwide for their richness in medicinal herbs, rhododendrons and primulas, while the temperate and subtropical belts are habitats for orchid species.

Table 2.1.Ten dominant families of flowering plants in Sikkim

Family	No. of species in India	No. of species in Sikkim	Per cent
Orchidaceae	1087	448	41
Compositae	1069	280	26
Graminae	1259	271	22
Leguminosae	1011	201	20
Cyperaceae	533	143	27
Rosaceae	492	138	28
Scrophulariaceae	423	112	26
Rubiaceae	659	110	17
Labiatae	452	95	21
Euphorbiaceae	528	94	21

Source: Singh and Chauhan, 1998

Sikkim has over 260 tree species in 158 genera and 70 families. Distribution of these tree species is influenced by climate, topography and elevation (Table 2.2). A study of the vegetation in various sites revealed that, in an area of 100 m^2, there are at least 58, 66, and 52 plant species in subtropical, temperate and alpine sites, respectively (Sundriyal, unpublished data). There are about 47 bird species in a small area of 4-5 km^2 in West Sikkim. However, Sikkim is under increasing biotic pressure. Some plant species are already listed in the Red Data Book.

In support of biodiversity conservation, the Himalayan countries have given legal protection status to many species of plants and animals. There currently are about 130 formal protected areas in the Himalaya, covering 13,600 km^2 (Zurick et al. 2005). They appear as national parks, wildlife preserves, conservation areas, and hunting reserves (Table 2.3).

Table 2.2 Life zones, vegetation and animals in the Sikkim Himalaya

Climatic zones	Vegetation			Animals	
	Climax species	Shrub species	Exotic species	Mammals	Birds
Alpine (>3800 m)	*Primula, Senecio, Sedum, Soxifraga, Potentilla, Gentiana, Pedicularis, Salix, Swertia, Ranunculus, Anemona, Juncus, Corydalis, Rheum, Pernassis, Arissema*	*Rhododendrons, Junipers, Meconopsis*		Snow leopard, Musk deer, Wild ass, Blue sheep, Marmot, Clouded leopard	Water fowl, Griffon, Vulture, Mountain finches, Brahminy duck
Sub-alpine (3000-3800 m)	*Abies webbiana, Latix grifithii, Picea Smithiana, Rhododendron hodgsoni, R. cinnabarium, Acer, Betula, Juniperus, Taxus buccata*	*Astragalus, Cotoneasiar, Arundinaria anstata*		Nayan, Bharal, Himalayan thar, Ghoral, Common leopard, Bear, Himalayan black beer Marmot	Impeyan pheasant, Tragopan, Osprey, Sunbirds
Cool-temperate (2700-3000 m)	*Quercus pachyphylla, Magnolia campbellii, Tsuge, Betula, Acer pectinatum, Michelia, Rhododendron*	*Rosa sericea, Princepia utilis, Arundinaria*	*Cryptomeria japonica*		Black eagle, snow pigeon, Tree sparrow, Blood pheasants, Hill partride, Magpies, Bluenapped pitta

Table 2.2. (Continued)

Zone					
Temperate (2000-2700 m)	Quercus lamellose, Castanopsis tribuloides, Machilus lanuginose, Symingtonia, Acer, Alnus nepalonsis, Macranga, Juglens	Leucoceptrum, Rubus, Smilex, Berberis	Pinus roxburghii, Eucalyptus	Langur, Barking deer, Gharal, Cloded serow, Leopard cat, Red panda, Marbled cat, Flying squirrel	Sunbirds, Monal pheasants, Emeral cuckoo
Warm temperate (1000-2000 m)	Mechilus edulis, Quercus lammeliosa, Q. lineate, Engalhardtia, Toona ciliate, Semecarpus, Eurya, Prunus, Castenopsis, Symplocos	Rubus, Oxyspora, Maesa, Cephalostichium			
Sub-tropical (<1000 m)	Shorea robusta, Terminalis, Castonopsis indica, Schima wallichii, Duabanga, Callicarpa, Syzygium, Leea, Dendrocalamus hamiltonii, Alianthes	Alstonia, Maesa, Spatholobus, Bauhinia	Delonix regia, Lagerstroemea parviflora, Jacranda	Jungle cat, Mongoose, Squirrels, Barking deer	Sparrows, Kites

Source: Rai and Sundriyal, 1997

In Sikkim, 40.65% of area (Khangchendzonga Biosphere Reserve 2619.92 km^2; Shingba Rhododendron Sanctuary 43 km^2; Kyognosla Alpine Sanctuary 31 km^2; FambongLho Wildlife Sanctuary 51.76 km^2; Barsey Rhododendron Sanctuary 104 km^2; and Maenam Wildlife Sanctuary 35.34 km^2) have been brought into protected area management network (Table 2.4). The two rhododendron sanctuaries, viz., Singba and Hiley-Barsey, are exclusively declared as protected areas keeping in view the commitments towards conservation of rhododendron species.

Table 2.3. The Himalaya: protected area and biodiversity

Parameters	Bhutan	Nepal	Indian Himalaya	Total Himalaya
Total Area (km^2)	46,500	140,800	425,000	612,300
Total Protected Area (km^2)	9,400	22,654	28,454	60,508
Threatened Mammal Species	12	17	29	58
Threatened Bird Species	3	2	5	10
Threatened Reptile Species	1	4	12	17
Plant Species	5,000	6,500	15,000	26,500
% Endemic Flora	10-15	33	35*	
Rare or Threatened Plant Species	5	15	1103	1123

*Figure is for the eastern Himalaya
Source: Zurick et al. 2005

The rhododendron habits of the terrestrial species were found to be of dwarf tussocks, small shrub or robust bushes which may sometimes form impenetrable and thickest at places. A large number of species grow as the epiphytes and only a few species grow to tree proportions (*Rhododendron arboretum, R. barbatum, R. falconeri, R. hodgsonii*) attaining heights up to 10-15 m. Rhododendrons form dominating species all along the cool temperate, sub-alpine and alpine zones in Sikkim Himalaya.

It is a keystone element and if disturbed can degrade habitats that threaten associated biodiversity. Restoration of rhododendrons and their conservation in nature promotes the existence of other biodiversity components.

Table 2.4. Biodiversity sensitive biosphere reserve, sanctuaries and other proposed areas in the Sikkim Himalaya

Park/ sanctuaries	Estab. (yr)	Area (km²)	Elevation (m)	Importance/specialties
Khangchendzonga Biosphere Reserve	2000	2655.26	1220 - 8550	Vegetational variation with elevation and wildlife. Most famous Yuksam-Dzongri-Goechha La trekking corridor of Sikkim. It is a notified biosphere reserve and a tourist destination.
Fambong Lho Wildlife Sanctuary	1984	51	1524-2750	Temperate vegetation and wildlife. This is a true representative of the sub-tropical eco-region and is rich in R. dalhousiae, bamboo forest and Oak. It is also a notified sanctuary and a tourist destination.
Maenam Wildlife Sanctuary	1985	35.34	NA	Vegetation and site seeing. Located in south Sikkim is a true representative of the Sub-tropical eco-region and is a very rich in R. griffithiannum and R. dalhousiae. Popular tourist destination.
Singba Rhododendron Sanctuary	1984	43	3300	This sanctuary above Lachung village, north Sikkim is a true representative of the temperate eco-region. R. niveum the state tree of Sikkim exists only in a small scattered population along with Abies webbiana Lindl. And other rhododendrons in protected areas. It is also a notified sanctuary and a popular destination for trekkers.
Kyongnosla Alpine Sanctuary	NA	31	3292-4110	Alpine vegetation and wildlife. Situated around the area adjoining the Chhangue lake along the Nathula road at a distance of about 31 km east of Gangtok in east district. The sanctuary is rich with wide variety of rhododendrons and rare and endangered medicinal plants.
Hilay-Barsey Rhododendron Sanctuary	NA	104	2200-4100	Well known for its unique abundance of rhododendron trees and shrubs. Part of Barsey rhododendron sanctuary has a triple junction where Singalila National Park of Darjeeling and eastern Nepal meet. R. arborium, R. cinnabarium, R. Falconeri, R. barbatum, R. campanulatum and R. hodgsoni are most common rhododendrons, which are found in the sanctuary.

Table 2.4. (Continued)

Park/ sanctuaries	Estab. (yr)	Area (km2)	Elevation (m)	Importance/specialties
Pangola	Proposed	108	1700-4500	Wildlife
Tolung	Proposed	230	1900-5100	sourWilderness
Dzongri	Proposed	468	2700-6700	High altitude vegetation
Kitam	Proposed	13	500-1000	Lower altitude vegetation and wildlife
Nimphu	Proposed	167	2500-5600	Temperate and alpine

NA= Not Available

Source: Rai and Sundriyal, 1997

Table 2.5. Important wildlife of protected areas of Sikkim Himalaya, and their threat categories from IUCN data

Common Name	Scientific Name	Ecological Zone	Local Name	Schedule/ part	Status
Barking Deer	*Muntiacus muntjak* Zimmermann	ST	Ratwa	III	T
Bharal	*Pseudois nayaur* (Hodgson)	AL	Nervati	I	V
Clouded leopard	*Neofelis nebulosa* Griffith	ST	Nigalay Chituwa	I	E
Common Langur	*Presbytis entellus* Dufresae	TE	Hanuman Bander	II/I	C
Ghoral	*Nemorhaedus goral* Hardwicke	TE	Himal ko goral	III	R
Great Tibetan sheep	*Ovis ammom hodgsoni* Blyth	AL	Tibet ko Bheran	I	E
Hill fox	*Vulpes v. Montana* Linn.	AL	-	-	-
Himalayan Black Bear	*Selenarctos thibetanus* (Cuvier)	TE	Konthe Bhalu	II/2	V
Himalayan thar	*Hemitragus jemlahicus* Smith	AL	Thar	I	E

Table 2.5. (Continued)

Common Name	Scientific Name	Ecological Zone	Local Name	Schedule/ part	Status
Himalayan yellow-throated marten	*Martes flavigula* Boddaert	ST	-	II	E
Indian porcupine	*Hystrix indica* kerr	ST	Dumsi	IV	C
Indian wild pig	*Sus scrofa* Linn.	ST	Bandel	III	IK
Marbled Cat	*Felis marmorata* Martin	TE	Jungali Biraloo	I	E
Musk deer	*Moschos charysogaster*	AL	Kasturi	I	E
Orange bellied squirrel	*Dremomyhs lokhriah* Hodgson	ST	Lotharkay	IV	C
Red Panda	*Ailurus fulgens* Cuvier	TE	Kudo	I	E
Serow	*Capricornis sumatraensis* (Bechstein)	AL	Thar	I	V
Snow leopard	*Uncia uncia* Schreber	AL	Semu	I	E
Tibetan wolf	*Canis lupus* Chanko	AL	-	II/2	V
Blood pheasant	*Ithagenus cruentus* (Hardwick)	AL	Chilimen	I	V
Crimson horned pheasant	*Tragopan satyra* (Linn.)	AL	Daphe	I	R
Forest eagle owl	*Budo nepalensis*	ST	Lat Kusyal	I	E
Himalayan golden eagle	*Aquila chrysaetosdaphanea*	AL	Sunaulo Giddha	I	E
Lammergeier	*Gypaetus barbatus*	AL	Budo Giddha	I	E
Monal pheasant	*Lophophorus impejanus* (Latham)	AL	Monal	I	E
Snow partridge	*Lerwa lerwa*	AL	Larewa	-	T
Snow pigeon	*Columba leuconata*	ST	-	-	T
Sparrow hawk	*Accipiter niscus*	ST	-	I	E
Tibetan snowcock	*Tetragaolus tibetanus*	AL	-	I	E
White breasted dipper	*Cinclus cinclus*	AL	-	I	R

Al= alpine, ST= sub-tropical, TE= temperate, E=endangered, V=vulnerable, T=threatened, C=common, R= rare

Primary direct threats to the Sikkim Himalaya's unique biodiversity are land-use/cover change, habitat degradation, extensive use of firewood, forest-fires and landscape fragmentation. Activities like grazing, unregulated tourism, road construction, unsustainable harvest of biodiversity products and poaching in some instances are the root causes of degradation and loss of biodiversity. About 65 plant species have been identified as threatened in the Sikkim Himalaya that includes many valuable medicinal plants (Appendix 1). As many species as 19 mammals and 11 birds are also threatened that includes animals like snow leopard, musk deer, red panda, Himalayan thar etc., and birds like blood pheasant, monal pheasant, sparrow hawk, forest edge owl etc. (Table 2.5).

The area has many transboundary issues within the two states (Darjeeling of West Bengal and Sikkim) of India, and between India and Nepal. The most prominent issues are transboundary grazing problem and movement of tourists in the two countries while trekking in the mountains. Grazers seem to know most of the valuable medicinal herbs and they are practicing unsustainable harvest. No compliance of code of conduct on environmental safeguard by travel agents of Darjeeling operating in Sikkim. Continuity of the borders over inhospitable areas has limited policing on poaching of bio-products.

2.2.1.1. Khangchendzonga Biosphere Reserve

In the Sikkim Himalaya, Khangchendzonga is a unique mountain ecosystem falling in three different national boundaries of India, Nepal and Tibet Autonomous Region of People's Republic of China (Fig. 2.1).

This mountain ecosystem encompasses sub-tropical to alpine zones housing a large number of flora and fauna and makes it a hotspot of biodiversity (Table 2.6). In this mountain ecosystem we find great variations in elevation, climate, landscape, habitat and vegetation types. It has a rich ethno-cultural diversity. The southern part of the Khangchendzonga Mountain Ecosystem comprises of eastern part of Nepal and Sikkim Himalaya.

In 2000, the Khangchendzonga national park was expanded and designated as the Khangchendzonga Biosphere Reserve. Khanchendzonga biosphere reserve is located in the district of North, South and West of the Sikkim state with a total area of 2655.26 km^2. It has two core zones with total area of 1819.34 km^2 and four buffer zones covering an area of 835.92 km^2. The biosphere reserve is in the altitude ranging from 1220 to over 8550 m asl. The detailed land-use/cover of the reserve is given in Table 2.7. The Yuksam-Dzongri trekking corridor is the main and famous trek route of Sikkim in KBR. It has 11 settlements with 274 households and a population of 1753. It is a trailhead for Dzongri, Thansingh, and Goche La, and a base camp for Khangchendzonga (the third highest mountain in the world) in Western Sikkim (Fig 2.2). The tourist trekking corridor extends over a distance of 26 km from Yuksam (the first capital of Sikkim) to Dzongri.

Table 2.6. Vegetation characteristics at different ecological zones of the Khangchendzonga Biosphere reserve

Ecological zones	Dominant vegetation		
	Tree	Shrub	Herb
Temperate-warm (1600-2000m)	*Castanopsis spp., Cedrela toona, Cinnamomum spp., Symplocos spp., Michelia lanuginos, Macaranga sp.,* etc.	*Rubus ellipticus, Edgeworthia gardneri, Oxyspora paniculata, Pentapanax sp., Girardinia dicursifolia, Melastoma normale, Casearia sp.,* etc.	*Eupatorium cannabinum, Cyanotis vaga, Hydrocotyle javanica, Pilea umbrosa, Impatiens sp., Brachiaria sp., Persicaria capitata, Plantago erosa,* etc.
Temperate-cool (2000-3000m)	*Rhododendron arboreum, Quercus lamellosa, Accer campbellii, A. Oblongum, Castanopsis tribuloides, Magnolia campbelli, Eurya acuminata,* etc.	*Maesa sp., Rubus paniculatus, Zanthoxylum acanthopodium, Daphne retusa, Aconogomum molle, Arundinaria maling, Viburnum spp., Caesaria sp.,* etc.	*Tupistra nutans, Viola sp., Silaginella sp., Elatostema sessile, Urtica dioica, Rumex nepalensis, Drymaria cordata, Diplazium umbrosum, Impatiens sp., Laportia terminalis, Ferns,* etc.
Subalpine (3000-3800m)	*Rhododendron barbatum, R. Hodgsonii, Abies densa, Betula alnoides, Acer sp., Tsuga dumosa,* etc.	*Rhododendron cinnabarinum, R. Wightii, Viburnum sp., Arundinaria maling, Rosa sericea, Daphne spp.,* etc.	*Potentilla spp., Selinum tenuifolium, Fragaria sp., Platystemma violoides, Prunella vulgaris, Gaultheria spp., Thalictrum sp., Primula spp.,* etc.
Alpine (>3800m)	-	*Rhododendron anthopogon, R. Lowndesii, R. Setosum, R. Lepidotum, R. Fulgens, Spiraea arcuata, Juniperus recurva, Rosa sericea,* etc.	*Aletris pauciflora, Primula spp., Potentilla spp., Rheum emodi, R. Nobile, Pedicularis spp., Gentiana spp., Saxifraga spp., Hemiphragma heterophyllum, Cassiope fastigiata, Poa spp., Anaphalis sp.*

Figure 2.1. Location map of Khangchendzonga Biosphere Reserve in Sikkim Himalaya.

Table 2.7. Land-use/cover (%) statistics of Khangchendzonga biosphere reserve

Land-use/cover class	Area	
	(km^2)	(%)
Mixed dense forest	478.68	18.02
Mixed open forest	180.84	6.81
Mixed degraded forest	172.32	6.49
Dense conifer forest	135.81	5.11
Open conifer forest	228.12	8.59
Degraded conifer forest	140.83	5.30
Oak-Rhododendron forest	62.81	2.37
Scrubs	28.59	1.08
Forest blanks	84.28	3.17
Alpine scrubs	244.79	9.22
Alpine pasture	20.62	0.78
Alpine barren	216.78	8.16
Snow	482.93	18.18
Glaciers	152.68	5.75
Lakes	4.28	0.16
River	13.42	0.51
Dry river bed	7.98	0.30
Total	2655.76	100

Source: Lepcha, 1998

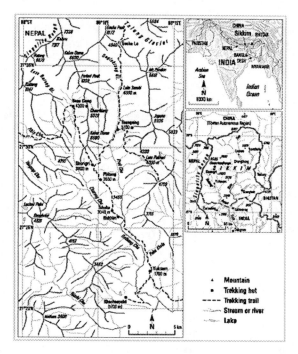

Figure 2.2. Location map showing the Yuksam-Dzongri trekking, Corridor in the Khangchendzonga Biosphere Reserve in Sikkim, (Chettri, et al., 2002).

The floristic wealth of the biosphere is rich and diverse, both in composition and value. The forests represent diverse plant communities which include diverse vegetational types corresponding to variation of climatic and edaphic factors. Species diversity, richness, and concentration are presented in Table 2.8. In the lower forest, tree species diversity was greater in the open canopy forest (H'=5.5) than in the closed canopy forest (H'=2.04), whereas in the upper forest, the pressure on forests was much lower, but secondary species had only a limited chance because of climatic constraints. Secondary species in open canopy forests played a major role in bringing about changes in species richness, concentration, and basal area (Chettri, et al. 2002). Only 43% of the total of 56 species in the lower forests was found to be regenerating in the closed canopy forests. Similarly, out of 32 species, 56% of the total in closed canopy forests and 58% in the open canopy forests were found to be regenerating in the upper forests. Secondary species such as *Symplocos ramosissima* and *Eurya acuminate* showed greater regeneration at almost all the sites (Chettri, et al. 2002). The faunal wealth is also equally rich in the reserve (Table 2.9).

Table 2.8. Species diversity, stand dimensions and regeneration in the lower forest and the upper forest along the Yuksam-Dzongri trekking corridor in Khangchendzonga Biosphere Reserve

Diversity Indices	Lower forest		Upper forest	
	Closed canopy	Open canopy	Closed canopy	Open canopy
Shannon-Welner's diversity Index (H')	2.04	5.52	2.8	2.5
Margalef's species richness (d)	5.4	8.8	4.2	4.7
Basal area (m²/ha)	59	23	50	40
Density (trees per hectare)	435	206	319	222
Tree species (number per site)	30	43	23	24
Regenerating species (number per site)	13	13	13	14
Regeneration (seedlings per hectare)	3480	2642	3694	2100
Regeneration (saplings per hectare)	1360	1200	860	585

Source: Chettri et al. 2002

Table 2.9. Distribution of faunal species in various categories

Fauna	Number of species
Mammals	
Alpine zone and Tibetan plateau	12
Timber line	4
Temparate zone	15
Sub-tropical zone	15
Birds	
Water fowls in the high altitude lakes	16
High altitude grassland birds	16
Forest birds in the treeline, temperate zone and sub-tropical zone	14

Source: Lepcha, 1998

Firewood and non-timber forest products (NTFPs) extraction along the trekking corridor has had distinct impacts on tree structure, regeneration of canopy tree species, and productivity of woody biomass. Table 2.10 presents the type and number of species of non-timber products (NTFPs) collected by local communities from the buffer zone of Khangchendzonga biosphere reserves (KBR). Compliance with the code of conduct for conservation by tourists, enterprises and communities especially concerning the use of alternatives to firewood, can help restore forests and make the destination more attractive and valuable.

Table 2.10. Types and number of species of non-timber forest products (NTFPs) collected by local communities from the buffer zones of the KBR

Non-timber forest products	Species Number
Construction and local handicrafts	8
Edible fruits and other products	41
Medicinal	31
Natural decorative	5
Fiber and broom species	3
Incense	2
Total	90

Forest-based resources are an integral part of the livelihood of people in the Hindu-kush Himalayan region. The Yuksam-Dzongri trekking corridor in the Khangchendzonga Biosphere Reserve of Sikkim is endowed with rich biodiversity. Lack of forest management scheme, unregulated tourism, and grazing has threatened the forest resources and biodiversity of this area for the past few decades. Extraction of firewood and timber for community use and tourism was observed all along the trekking corridor, although it was more pronounced near the major settlement of Yuksam.

2.3. DATA AVAILABILITY

Increasing concern on biodiversity loss and reporting requirements of international biodiversity agreements have called for world's attention to inventory and monitor the wealth of biodiversity. Yet, to date, only a few biodiversity data and information are widely available. Part of the reason is that the terrestrial and aquatic ecosystems of planet earth encompass enormous variety of biodiversity resources, thus making it challenging, time consuming and expensive to inventory and monitor all resources on Earth. Moreover, the available data are insufficient, scattered, and often incompatible to each other. A comprehensive review of the available data and information is necessary to see how well the available biodiversity data is reflected on the statistical and biological representations.

These dataset are available in different data formats such as numeric, categorical (classified or coded non- numeric data), text, spatial (map and GIS data), remote sensing (photographs and drawings), and sounds (e.g. voice of certain animal species).

2.3.1. Conservation Areas Data

There are currently about 30,350 protected areas in the world covering more than 13.23 million km^2 i.e. about 8.83% of the land on Earth (Green and Paine, 1997). Of these, 2,149 protected areas (2.5 million km^2) are known to have at least some marine element, of which 824 are island-protected areas. A comprehensive list of these protected areas can be found in "the 1997 United Nations List of National Parks and Protected Areas" (IUCN, 1998).

India has created a network of protected areas in the form of 84 national parks, 447 wildlife sanctuaries and 23 tiger reserve under the Indian Wildlife (Protection) Act of 1972. The areas covered under protected area network is 1, 48,000 km^2 which accounts for 4.5% of the total geographical area of the country. The other laws that have been evolved to strengthen the efforts for conservation of natural resources and for protecting the environment include: (i) The Water (Prevention and Control of Pollution) Act, 1974; (ii) The Forest (conservation) Act, 1980; (iii) The (Prevention and Control of Pollution) Act, 1981, and (iv) The Environment (Protection) Act, 1986. All these efforts aimed at to preserve the wildlife, a particular species or a particular community of animals and plants and their habitats rather than protecting the ecosystems and the rich genetic diversity contained therein (Rai, 1998).

The Man and Biosphere program (MAB) is guided by the MAB International Coordinating Council consisting of 34 Member States elected by the UNESCO General Conference. Programme activities are conducted in more than 100 countries under the direction of MAB National Committees or focal points. As of December 1999, there are about 357 MAB reserves worldwide. Biosphere reserves are alternative types of protected areas designed primarily for "in situ" conservation of natural and semi-natural areas, sustainable management of natural resources for local people, scientific research and monitoring, and environmental education and training. The MAB Programme is an interdisciplinary programme of research and training intended to develop the rational use and conservation of the resources of the biosphere, and to improve global relationship between people and the environment. A detailed list of the Man and Biosphere Reserves can be found at the UNESCO Biosphere Reserve Directory at http://www.unesco.org /mab/bios1-2.htm.

There are about 1,011 Ramsar wetlands covering an area of over 71.8 million hectares. These areas as designated following The Convention on Wetlands, signed in Ramsar, Iran, in 1971. The Convention's mission is "the conservation and wise use of wetlands by national action and international cooperation as a means to achieving sustainable development throughout the world". Detailed information on the Ramsar sites can be found at www.ramsar.org.

Currently, there are about 582 "World Heritage Sites" of which 445 are cultural, 117 are natural, and 20 are of mixed types. These areas are classified as "outstanding universal value" with the principal aim of fostering international cooperation in safeguarding these important sites. World Heritage lists are established following the convention concerning the protection of the world cultural and natural heritage in Paris in 1972. Detailed information of these sites are available at UNESCO's official website www.unesco.org/whc/heritage.htm.

2.3.2. Species Data

Species information is considered as the basic unit of documenting and describing biological diversity. This is supported by sound theoretical as well as operational reasons (Stanton and Lattin, 1989). Microbiologists, however, are in disagreement with this approach that highlighted the importance of having a different approach in defining biodiversity. Serious attempts are in place to use alternative basis for measuring biological diversity. It is extremely difficult to inventory all the species on Earth. This is the reason why the exact number of species on Earth is unknown. A conservative estimate ranges from 3 to 100 million species. For practical purposes, a total of 12.5 million species has been estimated as the known species. Out of this, only 1.7 million species have been described. This figure suggests that only 13% of species on Earth have yet been described. Furthermore, comprehensive catalogues of all 1.7 million species are not available and are poorly known in biological terms. The available information, in some cases, is inaccurate and biased. Inaccurate because it contains errors of taxonomic judgment and biased because a detailed and relatively accurate information is available only for some groups.

Continental distribution of these described species (global total) shows that Africa, Asia and the Pacific, and Latin America has the highest biodiversity.

Moist tropical forests cover approximately 8% of the world's land surface but holds more than 90% of the world's species. The information on species richness would consist of a complete catalogue of all the species occurring in the country or area under consideration. In practice, this is extremely difficult to achieve. Species composition changes through time and majority of the species are very small and are difficult to identify and count *in situ*. Moreover, collecting and counting all micro-organisms even for a small area is extremely difficult. For this reason, country species diversity data are predominantly available for mammals, birds, reptiles, amphibians, freshwater fishes, flowering plants, conifers and cycads, ferns and higher plants. In practice, overall species counts tend to be used for terrestrial vertebrates (mammals, birds, reptiles, amphibians), for some group of fishes and for few well-known invertebrate groups such as butterflies and dragonflies. Under such circumstances, information on endemism, which refers to a species confined entirely to that area or country, is important in relation to its importance in a wider context. Out of 250,000 flowering plant species, around 200 have been domesticated as food plants of which 25-30 are a crop of major world importance, judged largely by global production and economic criteria. FAO 1984 data suggest that there are more than 100 species that are significant at the national level. However, this database does not cover crops from home-gardens and data from many countries are missing.

2.4. MAJOR INTERNATIONAL CONVENTIONS

The following sub-sections provide brief descriptions on the major international conventions.

IUCN: The World Conservation Union

The World Conservation Union (founded in 1948) brings together states, government agencies and a diverse range of non-governmental organizations in a unique world partnership covering 81 countries, having its headquarters in Gland, Switzerland. IUCN seeks to influence, encourage and assist societies throughout the world to conserve the integrity and diversity of nature and sustainable use of natural resources. The World Conservation Union builds on the strengths of its members, networks and partners to enhance their capacity and to support global alliances to safeguard natural resources at local, regional and global levels.

International Status of Biosphere Reserves Network

The concept of biosphere reserve was evolved by UNESCO in 1974. The BR network was formally launched in 1976 and by March 1995, 352 BRs in 87 countries had been included in international network. Much of the action plan endorsed by UNESCO in 1984 remains valid today but the context in which BRs operate has changed considerably in the light of the Convention on Biological Diversity. The BRs remain under the sole sovereignty of the concerned country/state where it is situated, and participated in world network is voluntary.

CBD: Convention on Biological Diversity

The Convention on Biological Diversity's objectives are "the conservation of biological diversity, the sustainable use of its components and the fair and equitable sharing of the benefits arising out of the utilization of genetic resources." The Convention is thus the first global comprehensive agreement to address all aspects of biological diversity: genetic resources, species, and ecosystems. It recognizes - for the first time - that the conservation of biological diversity is "a common concern of humankind" and an integral part of the development process. To achieve its objectives, the Convention - in accordance with the spirit of the Rio Declaration on Environment and Development - promotes a renewed partnership among countries. Its provisions on scientific and technical cooperation, access to genetic resources, and the transfer of environmentally sound technologies form the foundations of this partnership. As of January, 2000, 176 countries have ratified the convention.

CMS: Convention on Migratory Species

The Convention on Migratory Species (CMS) aims to protect those species of wild animals that migrate across or outside national boundaries. This includes conservation of terrestrial, marine and avian species over the whole of their migratory range. The convention was concluded in 1979 and came into force on 1 November 1983. As of December 1999, 68 states have ratified the convention.

CITES: The Convention on International Trade in Endangered Species of WildFauna and Flora

CITES, is an international treaty drawn up in 1973 to protect wildlife against overexploitation and to prevent international trade from threatening species with extinction. The treaty entered into force on 1 July 1975 and now has a membership of 146 countries.

Ramsar Convention: Convention on Wetlands of International Importance

The Convention on Wetlands, signed in Ramsar, Iran, in 1971, is an intergovernmental treaty that provides the framework for national action and international cooperation for the conservation and wise use of wetlands and their resources. There are presently 117 Contracting Parties to the Convention.

Under the Ramsar Convention, 19 wetlands in India have already been declared (upto 2004) as Ramsar sites, while 12 more sites are under consideration with the Ramsar Secretariat.

The World Heritage Convention

The Convention Concerning the Protection of the World Cultural and Natural Heritage (the World Heritage Convention) was adopted by the General Conference of UNESCO in 1972. As of October 1999, more than 158 countries have signed the convention. This is one of the most universal international legal instruments for the protection of the cultural and natural heritage.

2.5. INTERNATIONAL EFFORTS

The following are the discussion on the major initiatives of generating and maintaining biodiversity data and information at the global level.

Bionet

BONET (Biodiversity Action Network) was established in 1993. BIONET aims "to help build international agreement among governments on concrete actions and targets needed to achieve the objectives of the CBD, with a special focus on forests and marine/coastal systems and to help catalyze specific national-level action to implement the CBD". Its mission is to advocate the effective implementation of the Biodiversity Convention worldwide, primarily through coordinated, joint NGO programs and information dissemination designed to catalyze governmental action.

Diversitas

Diversitas programme of IUBS (International Union of Biological Sciences), SCOPE (the Scientific Committee on Problems of the Environment) of the International Council of Scientific Unions (ICSU) and UNESCO was initiated in 1992. DIVERSITAS attempts "to inventorying and monitoring of biodiversity at the global level". It has 3 main themes: (i) inventorying and monitoring of overall biodiversity at all levels from genes to ecosystems incorporating both marine and terrestrial ecosystem; (ii) identify scientific issues and promote research requiring international coordination on the ecosystem function of biodiversity, the origins, maintenance and the practical consequences of current changes on the natural and managed ecosystems that support mankind; and (iii) develop prioritized agendas for research.

Forest Resources Assessment (FRA)

FRA-2000 of Food and Agricultural Organization of the United Nations aims to perform a global analysis of the distribution of forest ecosystem. Forest resources assessment and deforestation data are available for 1980 and 1990 in a country by country basis.

GBIF

The Global Biodiversity Information Facility (GBIF) was proposed by the OECD Mega science Forum working group on biological informatics subgroups for biodiversity informatics. The broad goal of the GBIF is to provide the most up-to-date and thorough biodiversity information in timely manner to policy- and decision makers, science and society, in all countries.

GTOS

The Global Terrestrial Observing System (GTOS) is a joint initiative by the FAO, WMO, UNEP, UNESCO and the International Council of Scientific Unions (ICSU). GTOS aims "to provide scientific coordinated, permanent, observational framework with adequate spatial coverage and temporal continuity to produce data to enable to detect, quantify, locate and understand changes in the capacity of terrestrial ecosystems to support sustainable development".

IOPI and Species 2000

The International Organization for Plant Information (IOPI) aims "to produce a checklist of the world's vascular plant species through a coordinated effort involving numerous specialists and institutions". IUBS in their 25th General Assembly in 1994 introduced SPECIES 2000 program the goal of which is "to provide a uniform and validated quality index of names of all known species for use as a practical tool". The index will be used to provide (i) an electronic baseline species list for use in inventorying projects worldwide; (ii) the index for an Internet gateway to species databases worldwide; (iii) a reference system for comparison between inventories; and (iv) a comprehensive worldwide catalogue for checking the status, classification and naming of species.

ISIS

The International Species Inventory System (ISIS) is a global network designed to (i) help the management of zoological collection; and (ii) enable zoos to meet their increasing conservation responsibilities. The ISIS maintains a centralized computer database of census, demographic, genealogical and laboratory data for wild species held in captivity.

Systematics Agenda 2000 International

SA 2000 is a proposal of discovery and research proposed by a Consortium of three international societies of systematic biologists: the American Society of Plant Taxonomists, the Society of Systematic Biologist and the Willi Hennig Society in cooperation with the Association for Systematic Collection. The Systematics Agenda 2000 International aims "to promote systematic/taxonomic research in all countries and regions in order to support ongoing activities to conserve and sustainably use their biodiversity". The main activities will be to develop international programs of systematic inventorying, phylogenetic research, the creation of systematic knowledge bases, and the promotion of systematic infrastructure and training.

2.6. INDIA'S BIODIVERSITY AND CONSERVATION

The number of species of different taxonomic groups, described from India is 47,000 species of plants and 89,000 species of animals, which contribute about 8% of the reported total number of species globally (Khoshoo, 1996; MOEF, 1999). About 33% of the flowering plants recorded in India are endemic to our country. Indian region is also notable for endemic fauna. For example, out of the recorded vertebrates, 53% fresh water fish, 60% amphibians, 36% reptiles and 10% mammalian fauna are endemic. The endemics are concentrated mainly in North-east, Western Ghats, north-west Himalaya and Andaman and Nicobar Islands.

The country is also rich in plants of medicinal importance. Nearly 3000 species have been mentioned in books dealing with medicinal plants, of which about 200 are used in bulk quantities for traditional systems of medicine, and plant products go into allopathic system from about 50 species (Jain and DeFilipps, 1991 cited in Sigh et al., 2006). Even species-poor localities may harbor a significant number of medicinal plants. Among the 25 hot spots of the world, two (Western Ghats and Eastern Himalaya) are found in India, and these extend into the neighboring countries also. However, anthropogenic pressures are affecting India's biodiversity as elsewhere. According to the 2003 Red List, in India, 45 plant species are critically endangered, 113 endangered and 88 vulnerable. Amongst animals, 19 are critically endangered, 54 endangered and 163 vulnerable.

India has taken significant steps for biodiversity conservation. As of 2004, India has 584 protected areas (92 national parks, and 492 wildlife sanctuaries), covering 4.735 of the land surface as against 10% internationally suggested norm. Five natural sites have been declared as "World Heritage Sites" which are KazirangaNational Park (Assam), KeoladeoNational Park (Rajasthan), Mans Wildlife Sanctuary (Assam), Nanda DeviNational Park (Uttarakhand), and SunderbansNational Park (West Bengal). The TuraRange in Garo hills of Meghalaya is a gene sanctuary for conserving rich diversity of wild Citrus and Musa species. Sanctuaries for rhododendrons and orchids have been established in Sikkim. The project Tiger was launched in 1973 and there are 25 tiger reserves spreading in 14 states (MOEF, 1999). Rhinos have been given special attention in selected sanctuaries and national parks in the North-east and North-west India. Similarly, several water bodies (e.g. Khecheopalri Lake in Sikkim) have been declared sacred by the people leading to protection of aquatic flora and fauna.

The Ministry of Environment and Forests, Government of India, has notified 13 biosphere reserves in India, which are also notified as National Parks. The Gulf of Mannar, Nilgiri and Sunderban are three biosphere reserves in India included in the list of the Man and Biosphere programme.

Chapter 3

GROWTH AND IMPACT OF TOURISM

3.1. INTRODUCTION

Tourism is now one of the most rapidly expanding sectors within the world's largest and fastest growing industry, and is emerging as a growing sector of economic development. The rapid and spectacular growth of tourism in the modern form is the main outcome of the increased mass demand for recreational facilities. This demand is the creation of the economic and social progress encouraged by scientific and technological achievements.The improvement in international and intra-national tourist facilities especially the introduction of chartered flights, increasing cheaper and variedtourist attractions have further stimulated and provided essential conditions for the growth of tourism (Singh, 1986). Tourism is regarded by many countries particularly resource poor-countries, as a potential stimulus to the economy. Yet tourism by the nature of the activities involved is considered by the natural resource base and infrastructure and by the pollution and other environmental and social impacts of tourist numbers (Brown et. al. 1997).

Large volume international tourism is primarily a phenomenon of the last fifty years and global mass tourism to develop on a large scale in the last two decades only. At global level the number of tourist arrivals has risen from slightly over 25 million in the 1950s to 443 million in 1990 (World Tourism Organization, 1991). The World Tourism Organization (WTO) reported that tourist activity in terms of number of visits has risen by 7% each year, with an increase of 12.5% in receipts, excluding international air fares. During the past decade there has been an average growth rate of 4% despite the world recession. The volume of tourists is still increasing, an increase which looks likely to continue over the next few decades (Hammed, 1993; cited in Brown et. al. 1997).

Mass tourism is not without disadvantages. The impact of tourism, on the environment and on local, social, economic and cultural life, is often detrimental. This has been documented in a range of countries both in the north and south, rich and poor nations. Therefore, it is important to assess not only the nature of motivation and attraction but also the feedback between them (Brown et. al. 1997).

Tourism is one of the most rapidly growing sectors of economic development with an estimated annual growth rate of 10-15% (Sreedhar, 1995 a &b). Since last two decades tourism sector has been a major growth sector and major source of employment. Tourism as an economic activity is becoming a common phenomenon in developing countries and possibly affects the livelihood of the poor, directly or indirectly. In fact tourism is generally viewed as engine for economic growth rather than as a mechanism for poverty reduction.

There are many researches that focus on tourism development from local, national and international perspectives, vis-à-vis the economic, social, cultural, political and environmental consequences (www.propoortourism.org.uk.2004). Moreover, there are studies that focus on tourism's contribution to foreign exchange earnings; the balance of payments and socio-economic development especially in developing countries. However, there is criticism on tourism development in developing countries due to high income leakages, environmental repercussions, and cultural impacts of tourism industry in these countries. Therefore, to overcome the negative effects of tourism, diverse forms of tourism development like rural tourism, community tourism, pro-poor tourism, and ecotourism are required. Despite the above arguments, it is a fact that tourism has already contributed much towards economic growth in both the developed and developing countries. Therefore, tourism is one of the viable alternatives to embark on economic development by reducing poverty and empowering the majority (Tadesse, 2009).

The magnificently diverse landscapes and rich cultural heritage of Sikkim in eastern Himalaya have contributed to the growth of tourism. In view of limited industrial growth in Himalaya, tourism can become a potential source of income generation in the remote mountain regions and generate employment opportunity for local people. Over recent years the area has experienced significant changes as a result of growth in tourism. Since 1990, there has been a tremendous increase in number of visitors in Sikkim Himalaya and its impacts and implications in the area are enormous. Sikkim is, thus, receiving more and more tourists but it has to bear a higher and higher environmental costs for each of tourists. Over the last 20 to 40 years, mountaineering and trekking have inflicted significant impacts upon high altitude area (Hinrichsen et al. 1983; Pawson et al. 1984; Karan and Mather, 1985; Banskota and Upadhyay, 1991; Stevens et al. 1991; Wells et al. 1991; Zurick, 1992; and Rai and Sundriyal, 1997).

This chapter describes growth of tourism pattern, visitor's profession, age-sex structure, income and expenditure pattern etc., market trend analysis related to tourism growth and impact of tourism.

3.2. DYNAMICS OF TOURISM GROWTH

India hosts nearly 2 million foreign visitors every year. Out of that only 0.3 to 0.4% visitors visited Sikkim. But the visitation number is increasing every year. The growth of tourist number in Sikkim has been showing an increasing trend from 1980s onwards. Until 1980, the state hosted only 10, 000 visitors, which eventually increased to more than ten times in 1997. The current tourist arrivals in Sikkim enumerate 251744 domestic and 16523 foreign tourists in 2005-06. It is expected that by the end of 20th century it may reach about half a million tourists per year, requiring a considerable increase in bed space capacity. But there is some indication of a decline in 1986 and 1987, due to Gorkha Land Movement in the adjoining Darjeeling hills of West Bengal (Fig. 3.1a). However, despite this steady increase the reason for visit seem hardly to have changed over several years. Khangchendzonga Biosphere Reserves is the most popular trekking destination in Sikkim Himalaya.The number of visitors visiting Sikkim is growing very fast during recent years. The main reason of this high growth in tourist influx was due to the relaxation in regulations that opened up a number of new areas for both foreign and domestic tourists.

Figure 3.1b illustrates that the state hosted the majority of domestic tourists in comparison to foreign visitors. The majority of domestic visitors are from West Bengal (65%), followed by Delhi (10%), Bombay (6%), Madras (5%) and the rest 14% from other parts of the country. The foreign visitors mainly came from UK (14%), Germany (13%), France (10%), USA (9%), Japan (6%), Switzerland (5%) and the rest 27% from other countries. More than 70% domestic and 35% foreign tourists visited Sikkim for recreational purposes, followed by 5% domestic and 60% foreigners for adventure (Rai and Sundriyal, 1997). The flow of visitors has two distinct peaks annually, with a high inflow during April-June and October-December, and low inflow in January-March and July-September. During spring and fall, Sikkim offers an ideal condition for recreation and trekking. Visitor numbers were recorded highest in the month of October to November and March to May. This is a pattern typical of most of the Hindu-kush Himalayan region. As a result, the physical flow of tourists and the financial flow of tourism earnings have been skewed to benefit the area, despite tourism's promotion as an economic panacea for the local community.

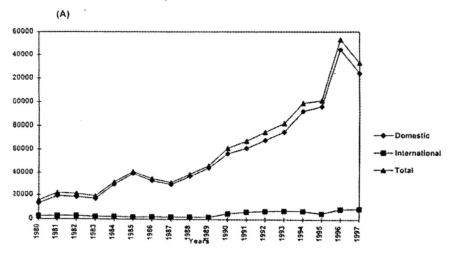

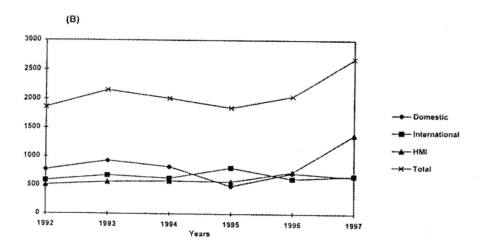

Figure 3.1. (A) Tourist arrivals in Sikkim (1980-1997), (B) Annual increase in number of adventure tourist in Yuksam-Dzongri-Goechha La trekking corridor of Sikkim (1992-1997).

3.2.1. Tourism Pressure

Most tourists (80.12%) intend to visit Tshangu lake, followed by Shingba Rhododendron Sanctuary (7%), Barsey Rhododendron Sanctuary (2.11%), Khangchendzonga Biosphere Reserve (1.41%), Fambong Lho Wildlife Sanctuary (0.83%) and Maenam Wildlife Sanctuary (0.60%) (Fig. 3.2) and these results in environmental problems, particularly on pollution and soil degradation. Figure 3.3 illustrate ten most important sites of attraction in the Sikkim Himalaya. Present experience suggests that if the numbers of tourists increase, pressure in the KBR, especially on the camp sites will reach unacceptable limits. In some months/seasons the number of visitors to the biosphere reserve exceeds the daily limit (Table 3.1).

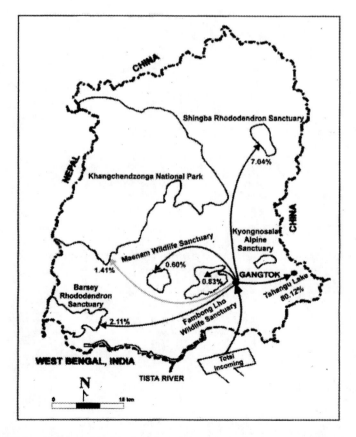

Figure 3.2. Visitors flows to National park and sanctuaries in Sikkim Himalaya.

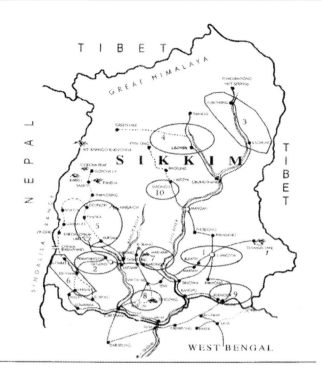

1. Gangtok,Rumtek & Changu (East)
2. Pelling, Pema yangtshe (West)
3. Lachung,Yumthang (North)
4. Lachen, Gorudongbar (North)
5. Yuksam, Dzongri(West)
6. Varsey, Uttarey (West)
7. Ravangla, Maenam (South)
8. Namchi, Samduptes (South)
9. Aritar Khedi & Pastanga (East)
10. Dzongu (North)

Figure 3.3. Map showing top ten tourist destinations of Sikkim Himalaya.

Table 3.1. Seasonal variations in number of adventure tourists in Sikkim Himalaya, 1997

| Seasons | Yuksam-Dzongri-Goechha La trail route | | | | | |
| | Domestic | | International | | HMI* | |
	Number	Group	Number	Group	Number	Group
Winter	6 (0.93)	2	18 (2.72)	7	315 (22.84)	5
Spring	35 (5.45)	7	146 (22.05)	30	342 (24.80)	5
Summer	287 (44.70)	37	145 (21.90)	37	351 (25.45)	6
Rainy	31 (4.83)	8	26 (3.93)	6	181 (13.13)	4
Fall	283 (44.08)	50	327 (49.40)	52	190 (13.78)	2
Total	642 (100)	104	662 (100)	132	1379 (100)	22
"t" value (0.05)	178	26.5	155.32	24.62	103.71	1.88

Values in parentheses are percentages; *HMI=Himalayan Mountaineering Institute.
Source: Rai, 2002

Sikkim experiences five seasons, the fall season, which runs from October to November, winter from December to February, spring from March to April, summer from April to May and the rainy season from June to September. In KBR there is a significant seasonal difference in the number of tourist arrivals.

3.2.2. The Nature of Adventure/Trekking Travel

Mountain trekking in the highland pristine forests and white water rafting are the main forms of adventure tourism in Sikkim. River rafting is relatively new in Sikkim. In 1994, only 200 rafters travelled the rivers, which increased to 465 in 1997.

Majority of the rafters went on the Tista River, which is most accessible from Gangtok. Mountain trekking is the most popular adventure activity in Sikkim (Table 3.2). Out of the total visitors, about 42% of visitors listed their main motivation to trekking. Trekking in Sikkim follows an age-old pattern of movement within the mountains. These are traditional migratory routes and seasonal encampments among highland pastures that were used for grazing the animals and upto some extent they now lead tourists' expeditions into the more remote areas. Metalled roads extend the traditional travel circuits for tourism purposes. Nature oriented tourism activity is also gaining momentum in recent years.

The Yuksam-Dzongri-Goechha La trekking corridor is the most popular trekking destination in Sikkim (Fig 3.4). Trekking travel in this trail started in 1960. A Kalimpong based tour operator as stated by local people arranged the first organized trek in 1973 (Maharana, 2000). Sikkim state opened its borders to foreigners in 1980. The rise of Sikkim popularity as an adventure travel destination began in 1990. Foreigners are allowed to go to trek only in groups. Foreign tourists need an entry permit to visit Sikkim as well as protected areas for a maximum duration 15 days. Tour operators arrange the visit and charge daily rates, including food and guides of between US$ 25 to 50 per person per day. Domestic tourists without involvement of travel agents independently organize their own treks. In the latter case, economic benefits may be dispersed more widely through the state, but local, social and environmental impacts are likely to be more pronounced. The organized trekkers, on the other hand exert direct pressure on the environment for more fuelwood requirement to large support staff, trailside erosion due to heavily laden pack animals and garbage problem at campsites. The HMI mountaineering team is more support intensive and causes heavy damage to campsites especially at high altitude.

Table 3.2. Identified trek routes of Sikkim Himalaya

Sl. No.	Name of Trek	Grade	Permit requirement DT (yes/no)	IT (yes/no)	Average duration from road
		NORTH SIKKIM			
1	Green Lake	Strenuous	Yes	Not Open	7 days
2	Tolung Monastery	Moderate to M. strenuous	Yes	Yes	1-2 days
3	Thangu- Chorten Nyima la	Strenuous	Not Open	Not Open	3 days
4	Gurudongmar	M. strenuous to Strenuous	Yes	Not Open	2-4 days
5	Lhasar Valley	Strenuous	Not Open	Not Open	5-7 days
6	Phimpu	Moderate	No	Yes	2 hrs
7	Samertek	Moderate to M. strenuous	Yes	Yes	3-5 days
8	Lava-Tarum tsa chu	M. strenuous	Yes	Yes	7 days
9	Tosa	Moderate	Yes	Yes	6 days
		SOUTH SIKKIM			
1	Rabongla-Maenam	Moderate	Yes	Yes	1-2 days
2	Chakung	Moderate	No	Yes	2 days
3	Damthang-Tendong	Moderate	Yes	Yes	1 days
		WEST SIKKIM			
1	Yuksam-Goechela	Moderate to M. strenuous to Strenuous	Yes	Yes	7-8 days
2	Uttarey-Singalila	Moderate to M. strenuous	Yes	Yes	9-14 days
3	Hilley-Varsey	Moderate	Yes	Yes	2 days
4	Monastic trek (W)	Gentle to Moderate	No	Yes	5 days
5	Soreng-Rinchenpong	Moderate	No	Yes	2 days
		EAST SIKKIM			
1	Assam Lingzey-Khedi	Moderate	No	Yes	3-4 days
2	Tinjure-Tumin	Moderate	No	Yes	1-2 days
3	Gangtok Walking Tour	Gentle	No	No	6-8 hrs
		INTER DISTRICT			
1	Monastic Trek (E & N)	Gentle to Moderate	No	Yes	3-4 days
2	MonasticTrek(E, S & W)	Gentle to Moderate	No	Yes	7 days

Source: Trekking Master Plan for Sikkim, 2000

The rise in Nepal's popularity as a destination for so-called "adventure travel" began in earnest during the 1970s, when Kathmandu was the terminus for overland trips from Europe. The rise in foreign tourists, increasing from only 6179 in 1962, to almost 300,000 in 1991, with increase in record numbers of visitors almost every year. The majority of these visitors are attracted to Nepal's natural resources: in 1988, approximately 20% of visitors came exclusively to trek in the mountains, and an additional 60% came for some combination of trekking, jungle safaris, river rafting or ethnic tourism (Zurick, 1992).

Figure 3.4. Trekkeing along Yuksam-Dzongri trial route.

There is some secondary evidence to suggest that the tourism cycle is being observed in Nepal. Zurick's study (Zurick, 1992) of variations in the number of trekkers to various parts of Himalaya shows a sequence similar to that proposed by Butler (1980). For example visitors to Annapurna, the most popular trekking destination, increased from 52% of all trekkers in 1980 to 68% in 1986. However, 1990 saw a drop in numbers back 60% of the total and Zurick claims this is because the area is commonly perceived to be overcrowded. Perception of environmental degradation and negative social and cultural impacts are reported and have perhaps affected people's decisions about which areas they visit and how long they stay in the country (Brown et al. 1997).

3.2.2.1. Pattern of Adventure/Trekking Travel

Sikkim's diverse natural and cultural heritage partially determines the level of tourism activity and type of programs found at specific localities. Other factors include advertisements by Government and tour operating agencies, government policies, and promotional efforts of local entrepreneurs. Sikkim opened its borders to foreigners in 1950, but not until the 1960s did many foreign tourists visit the area. The increasing number of visitors to Sikkim began in 1990, due to relaxation in regulations. The period 1992-97 showed a steady rise in the number of tourists who entered for trekking purposes (Fig. 3.1.b). In 1997, about 2000 visitors came exclusively to trek in the high mountains in Yuksam-Dzongri-Goechha La trail route. The HMI conducted 8 training courses every year consisting of 1379 trainees. The magnitude of adventure travelers in Yuksam-Dzongri-Goechha La route exemplifies the importance of seasonality factors. The area is crowded particularly during summer and the fall trekking season (Table 3.1). It is clear from Table 3.3 that most of the trekkers visit Sikkim to observe the beauty of nature and experiencing wilderness (Fig 3.5).

Table 3.3. Reasons for visiting Sikkim Himalaya

Reasons	Visitors			
	Domestic		International	
	No	%	No	%
Holiday/pleasure	36	20.33	73	30.67
Trekking/mountaineering	123	69.49	155	65.13
Religious purpose	10	5.65	7	2.94
Any other	8	4.52	3	1.26
Total	177	100	238	100

Source: Rai, 2002

Figure 3.5. View of snowclad mountains from Dzongri is one of the major attraction for the tourists.

Due to the significance of trekking for Sikkim's tourism development, the state is upgrading its trekking objectives in recent years, including calls for the diversion of tourists into newly opened areas.

The tourists who visited the Yuksam-Dzongri-Goechha La trail are mainly classified into four categories on the basis of daily expenditure for food and services while in trek. Table 3.4 revealed the relative frequency of each tourist category, the average length of stay, the average daily expenditure, and the proportion of total visitor's days. Table 3.4 reveals that the major source of tourist-related income is from luxury tourist group. The members of HMI represent significant contribution to the overall picture of tourist activity in the area since beginning. They frequently employ hundred of pack animal porters to carry food and equipment from Yuksam to base camp. The HMI route is same up to Tshoka and then diverts and comes close to Dzongri from the south side, and it goes up to base camp.

Table 3.4. Adventure visitors by tourist category, length of stay and daily expenditure, 1997

Tourist category	Relative frequency	Average length of stay (days)	Average daily expenditure (US $)	Proportion of total visitor days (%)
Luxury	27.77	15	45	42.85
Standard	42.22	10	35	28.57
Economy	26.66	5	20	14.28
Budget	3.33	5	5	14.28
Total/Avg.	100	8.75	26.25	100

Source: Rai, 2002

It was observed that the tourist below the age of 20 years constitute only 1%, while above the age group of 60 have been also estimated 1% each. The percentage of male visitors had been higher than the female for both domestic and international visitors mainly due to difficult terrain and inaccessibility. The principal mode of travel to the trekking site by all types of visitors was reserved taxi, followed by shared taxi and least by government run buses.

During the survey, it was observed that bulk of domestic and foreign visitors took accommodation in tourist huts, followed by tent and hotel/lodges (Fig 3.6). Presently more than 50% of the domestic and foreign visitors are staying in hotels at Yuksam. The per capita per day expenditure of the tourist is an important factor having economic significance. Majority of the domestic tourists belonged to the lower-middle (Rs. 2000 to Rs. 6000) and middle class (Rs 6000 to Rs 10,000) income groups. In case of the foreign visitors, they belonged to the middle and upper middle class (Rs. 10,000 to Rs. 20,000) (Maharana, 2000). The major source of tourist related income was from organized treks.

Figure 3.6. Tourists camps at Tshoka on the trail.

3.2.2.2. Visitors Opinion and Reaction

About the opinion of the 'Food', majority of the domestic and foreign visitors considered it as "Good" in quality as well as in taste, whereas lack of good restaurants at Yuksam has also been noted. When asked about the accommodation facility, most of the visitors stated that it was just about "Average". The trekker huts were over-crowded during peak tourist season and camping at sites are generally observed.

The general opinion of visitors about the local people is very satisfactory. Both domestic and foreign visitors consider local people as "hospitable". Overall, the visitors were satisfied with the assistance and facilities provided by tourist information centre as well as tour operators.

A considerable number of the visitors strongly showed their discontentment about the condition of the trail. Most of the both types of visitors frequently mentioned about the litter along the trail and campsite. In general, most of the visitors expressed their satisfaction about the local hospitality and food. However, a few visitors were disappointed during stay in trekker's huts. As a whole majority of the domestic and foreign visitors were satisfied with the site appearance. For a sustained rate of growth of the tourist industry, the complaints, however, deserve urgent attention and remedial measures.

3.3. TOURISM IMPACTS

Evidence shows that severe degradation of the environment has occurred in the trail route and some parts of Sikkim as a result of tourism. The impacts of tourism are many and require local people awareness and participation to solve the problems. If visitor number increases and is more concentrated on a small area then impacts upon resources and physical environment will be more severe. The impacts on host region are not only negative but it has positive impacts also. In the trekking corridor, the major impacts are trailside litter, forest cutting for fuelwood and construction, overgrazing by Yak/Dzo and pack animals, trailside erosion is commonly observed throughout the trailhead.

3.3.1. Negative Impacts

3.3.1.1. Fuelwood Use
It is obvious that local communities, visitors and their support staff attribute much of the environmental damage to tourist related activities, particularly the use of firewood. However, deforestation originated long before the advent of tourism in the area (Fig 3.7). House construction and increased need for fuelwood and fodder contributed to the gradual depletion of forest resources. A survey of households in the Yuksam village showed that a double-storied building/lodges needs about 600 to 700 ft^3 wood, and even a small house needs at least 400 ft^3 wood (Rai and Sundriyal, 1997). Before the adoption of strict fuel use regulation, it was estimated that the local communities consumed about 6200 kg of fuelwood per day, followed by hotel/lodges 274kg per day, and 2 to 10 kg per day by supporting staff (Table 3.5). A large quantity (about 240 kg per day per group) of fuelwood is used by HMI people during training courses, for cooking and water heating. The supporting staffs of tour operators were often using fuelwood for cooking, and not necessarily obeying existing regulations regarding the compulsory use of kerosene by trekking groups. At the 1997 population level, the total fuelwood requirement in Yuksam village native population was about 2264 Mg/year. The total fuelwood consumption calculated as above could be considered as the demand or pressure on the surrounding forests. The greater extraction of fuelwood (919 Mg/year) was estimated in Dubdi forest, followed by

522 Mg/year in KNP trail, 489 Mg/year in Chihan Dara and 434 Mg/year in Pahakhola Thaktu forest. The assumption underlying this calculation is that àll the fuelwood required is supplied from the forest.

Figure 3.7. Habitat degradation along the trail are responsible for trail erosion.

Table 3.5. Seasonal variation of fuelwood consumption by different stakeholders in Yuksam-Dzongri-Goechha La corridor of Sikkim Himalaya

Stakeholders	Consumption (tons)			Average ($Mg\ d^{-1}$)	Annual ($Mg\ y^{-1}$)
	Summer (61 days)	Rainy (122 days)	Winter (182 days)		
Community	378.32	756.64	1128.76	6.20[1]	2263.72
Hotel/lodges	16.72	33.45	49.90	0.27[2]	100.07
HMI	2.30	13.07	28.51	0.24[3]	100.07
Travel Agent	0.16	3.40	3.56	0.010[4]	7.12
FITs	0.65	0.0	1.30	0.001[5]	1.95
Pack-animal Operator	0.086	0.41	0.53	0.002[6]	1.026
Porter	0.28	6.25	8.85	0.002[7]	15.38

1,2: community and hotel consumption per day; 3,4: per group; 5,6,7: per person.
Source: Maharana, 2000

Trekking travel also played an important role in the change to pastoralism in the Yuksam area. During the past one decade emphasis was given to Yak/Dzo rearing. The total livestock population of Yuksam block was 1557 in 1997. The Yak/Dzo and cattle need about 35 kg of green fodder per day and a sheep and goat needs about 15 kg per day. Such large amount of fodders is supplied from the neighboring forest areas along the trail route.

3.3.1.2. Trail Erosion

The Yuksam-Dzongri-Goechha La trail route is facing serious trail erosion problem during the rainy season, resulting from excessive wood cutting, over use because of hiking and heavy grazing. The overland flow (percentage of rainfall during rainy season) was estimated to be the highest in degraded forest (5.76%), followed by open missed forest (2.91%), trail side (1.84%) and the lowest in alpine pasture (higly grazed 0.93% and low grazed 0.21%)). The soil loss was also recorded highest in degraded forest (122 kg/ha), followed by open mixed forest (25 kg/ha) and lowest in alpine area (highly grazed 1.85 kg/ha and low grazed 0.99 kg/ha) (Table 3.6). This high rate of soil erosion is mainly due to depletion of ground cover, excess use of forest resources, increase in visitor inflow, and heavily laden porters (pack animals) (Fig 3.8).

Figure 3.8. Pack animal used as porterage by tourists along trekking route.

Table 3.6. Impact of tourism on landscape environment along Yuksam-Dzongri trekking trail

Land-use/landscape	Area (%)	Overland flow (% of rainfall)	Soil loss (kg/ha)
Highly grazed	-	0.93	1.85
Low grazed	-	0.21	0.99
Trail side	-	1.84	37.17
Dense mixed forest	14.10	1.70	10.20
Open mixed forest	25.05	2.91	25.46
Degraded forest	10.24	5.76	121.46
Large cardamom based agroforestry	-	0.22	2.65
Cropped area	-	0.21	2.97
Barren land	0.64	0.73	26.98

(-) Not available

3.3.1.3. Solid Waste

Littering of non-biodegradable material on the trail route is a common problem because of the large number of people using the trail (Fig 3.9).

Figure 3.9. Non-biodegradable garbage disposal near a campsite on the trail.

Improper disposal of solid waste is also playing an important role to degrade the environment. Despite the Biosphere reserve, visitors remove bushy trash, and trails and campsites are becoming increasingly littered. Waste disposal has continued to be the eyesore along the main trekking route. Garbage and litter collections have been a major problem in the route. Government regulations have required the trekking groups to pack-out their waste, but very few groups follow this rule. The result has been a continuing accumulation of trash along the trail. In 1996, a recently formed local NGO has organized a cleaning campaign in the trail route and they collected huge amount of litter i.e., 50 kg of plastic bags, 100 kg empty can fruit juice and 100 kg of bottles during fall season. The increasing proliferation of plastic, metal, and glass has been exacerbated not only by careless disposal of trash, but also by the increased non-biodegradable litter.

3.3.1.4. Socio-Cultural

Due to the mass tourism growth, the socio-cultural consequences are considerable. In this area cultural changes have resulted due to fusion of different cultures and people. It is very difficult to determine or to measure, but the effects of exceeding the limit are quite obvious. Social inequality increases, values change and life styles shift. Sikkimese is proud of their cultural heritage. Sikkimese festivals and monasteries have attracted international recognition. A good deal of the new affluence from tourism has been spent in affirming faith. Restoration and expansion of monasteries and introduction of other religious sites have been increased in recent years in Yuksam. The uneven distribution of economic benefits increased status and power to men from formerly poor and low status households in the village society. The other social problems like children begging for money and sweets and improper dress offending local customs were observed in the area during our fieldwork. It is clear that overall social impacts are serious threats for the uniqueness of the region. Change, however, is inevitable when local populations embrace the tourist system.

3.3.2. Positive Impacts

3.3.2.1. Economic Benefits

Growth of visitor's number has been responsible for significant changes in employment and income generation, which lead to improve living standards of the local people and overall national and state economic development. In economically depressed areas, the employment and income provided by tourism may help to check out-migration. Increased government revenues, through various types of taxation on tourism can be used to develop community and infrastructure facilities and services in the region. Despite the high royalty being charged (US$ 8 per trek) none of the money received from trekking tourism has yet been properly invested by the government in the area. The indirect economic benefit of tourism is that it serves as a catalyst for the development or expansion of other economic sectors, such as agriculture, construction, and handicrafts, through their supplying the goods and services used in tourism.

The people of Yuksam village have reoriented their local economy around tourism. In 1996, about 49% of the total households had income from this source. Since then, involvement in tourism related activities has risen to 60% within a span of one year, and it has become increasingly common to involve tourism-related activities. Most of the income (53%) came from employment in trekking and mountaineering as porterage (US $ 38574/year), followed by grocery shop (US $ 12526/year), guided tour (US $ 12180/year), hotel/lodges/tea stall (US$ 9126/year excluding the income of one three-star hotel), and very minimum to local guides (US$ 607/year) in 1997. Employment in both trekking and mountaineering is seasonal. Hotel/lodges have become an increasingly important part of the regional as well as local economy. Hotel/lodges are the most profitable business. Yuksam village has 5 hotel/lodges (including one three-star hotel) and then earned about (US $ 19897) in 1997, two times more than 1996 directly into the Yuksam economy. It is often said that the economic gains from adventure tourism are more quickly distributed throughout the regional as well as local economy than other types of tourism. This proved by the fact that much of the gains derive from accommodation and porterage.

3.3.2.2. Increasing Environmental Awareness

Due to increasing trends of adventure/trekking travelers in the area, and training program organized by Sikkim Biodiversity and Ecotourism project since 1996, the local community members are more aware about their environment and cultural heritage, realizing the importance of conservation to the economic success of the area. Impacts of these training programs were highly successful and that was proved by the fact that Friends' of Nature, a Kolkata based environment organization that trekked through this route, has applauded the state Government's role in the protection of environment in this trail route. In a letter addressed to the President of India, the organization has highlighted the role of general public, guides, porters and government in the state for their efforts in environmental protection. They have remarked that protection of environment in Sikkim especially in Yuksam area was exemplary and requested the President to issue instructions to all other state Governments to follow Sikkim's example.

3.3.2.3. Improvement of Infrastructure

Tourism plays an important role in the development of infrastructure like roads, water supply, sewage, and solid waste disposal system and telecommunications. These facilities are improved due to increase in adventure/ trekking travelers. Transport facilities have increased. In 1995, there was only one bus and taxi service available for Geyzing on irregular basis. But in 1997, 2 buses and 5 private owned taxies were running in between Geyzing, Gangtok and Jorethang on regular basis.

The Himalaya is not only mountain region experiencing problems with the management of trekking tourism. Newly popular trekking routes in Africa, particularly in the Rwenzori range (Mountains of the Moon) and Mount Kilimanjaro are already becoming over-used and eroded. Visitor numbers on the Inca Trail to Mchu Picchu in Peru, now one of the most famous trekking routes in the world, have increased by 800% over the past decade, causing serious problems with trail deterioration. These are compounded by poor and ineffective management, combined with commercial pressures from trekking agencies and local communities. Around 40, 000 visitors per year now walk the trail, together with large numbers of porters and guides (Shackley, 1999). Similar experiences were also observed in Semen Mountain National Park of Ethiopia. In 1991 the SMNP received only 54 foreign tourists, which increased to 6500 in 2008 walk the trail (Tadesse, 2009). The resulting impacts include: (i) trail damage from excess visitors and heavily-laden porters wearing out the steep masonry stairs and pathways; (ii) infamous litter and pollution problems, with no facilities for waste disposal; and (iii) dirty and overcrowded campsites with few sanitary facilities. Problems are made worse by the lack of a coherent administration policy.

These studies indicate that perhaps the ecological carrying capacity of these fragile mountain ecosystems has been exceeded. Whilst such impacts are fairly direct, and are caused by the increasing pressure of burgeoning numbers of tourists, other impacts may be more indirect. For example, Yonzon and Hunter (1991) discuss the habitat destruction caused by unsustainable farming practices used to produce cheese, a high-value product demanded by tourists in Lantang National park of Nepal.

3.4. TOURISM MARKETING

3.4.1. Tourism Operations

The commercial basis and business structure of ecotourism has been identified, which observes that ecotourism: (i) Is a labour and knowledge intensive industry; (ii) Is young and so its community is not well organized like mass tourism; (iii) Often uses focused or targeted marketing methods, networking, and guide books to sell products; (iv) Originates from an interest in the environment- it sells a product which celebrates nature and seeks understanding and experience of natural systems.

For the "Sensitive" and "contributory" providers of nature based ecotourism, the business of tourism is not always, and in some instances rarely, a moneymaking venture. The per capita expenses of nature based ecotourism are higher than high-volume or mass tourism because of the small group sizes, remoteness, additional equipment, expensive transportation, need for an expert or specialist guide and the cost of contributing towards the resource (Preece and Oosterzee, 2007, in htpp:// www.environment.gov.au). Tour operations are privately owned, and agencies are often run by the original founder. By and large, product decisions are based on personal preferences. In considering the role of industry in biodiversity conservation, all segments of the nature-based and ecotourism industry should be addressed. The accommodation and transport sectors are intimately connected with these activities, as they are indeed for tourism in general.

3.4.2. Products and Marketing

For a marketing perspective, nature based and ecotourism is about packing a different product, to a different audience, with different results from that of mass tourism. By understanding the customers, their motivations and characteristics, decision-makers can better create tourist packages, bring in more money, manage tourism impact and contribute to conservation of biodiversity.

Sikkim does not have visibility in the market compared to other Himalayan destinations such as Nepal, Bhutan, Ladakh and Tibet. In addition there is a general vague notion in the market that Sikkim is difficult to get into and that permits are difficult to obtain. There is little coverage on Sikkim in the press media. Internationally, there is practically no awareness of Sikkim as an ecotourism adventure travel destination in comparison to other Himalayan adventure destinations.

Sikkim's most conspicuous attraction is its excellent biodiversity. This is what sets Sikkim aside from other Himalayan destinations. In addition Sikkim Kargu and Ningmapa Monasteries are located at trail route and have an ancient history and the art has largely been well preserved in several monasteries. The monastic culture is well preserved and has not been well exposed to the international market. Currently one/two agents are selling diversified trek products in Nepal and Bhutan as well as Tibet in order to be able to have a year round offer of products.

Maintenance and promotion of natural, social and cultural diversity is essential for long term sustainable tourism and creates a resilient base for industry. In most of the areas there is a lack of tourism promotion in general and trekking in particular. Lack of promotional measures in Sikkim is a great hindrance for selling its products. Presently the promotional activities adopted by Sikkim based tour operator is advertising in only Indian Newspapers and Magazines, selling to direct walk-in clients, a few operators with proven service are handling referral business from Nepal, a few operators handling business from foreign individual motivations and agents. A good quality brochure would be of most important for tourism marketing.

In 1997-98 survey of tour operators identified the six most popular products/most popular activities offered. Due to the customers' "need" to continually explore new areas, new products are continually developed. This may mean opening new destinations. New destinations, and new packages for old destinations, are motivated by visitors, tour operators and tourism agencies. Visitors demand may increase for a particular location due to news coverage or a popular film. A location may also become popular because of the rising interest in the activities offered. While adventure and nature travel is big business, there is a very personal component to how decisions are made. The travel business, nature travel included, is reportedly very competitive with slim margins. It is also an industry of privately-owned businesses where agencies and firms are run by the founders who are generally intimately involved with the choice of destinations and how business is conducted. Most of the tour operators are small except few in Sikkim. Consequently, many product decisions are based on personal preferences as well as a dispassionate analysis of the market place.

Travel agents represent a key interface in the tourism marketing system (Bitner and Booms, 1982). In addition to helping travelers book reservations and obtain tickets and vouchers, they influence tourism planning decisions and outcomes. The major tour operators in Sikkim use ordinary marketing techniques, relying mainly on the use of brochures. Tour operators are not very knowledgeable about their customers and the market segment they serve. They recognize that customers are buying "experience" – not products, as this selection of advertising materials. The high percentage of tour operators that use magazines and brochures demonstrates that operators are carefully targeting their customers and also relying heavily on requests for information. Nature travel products must adapt to the changes in preferences brought about by shifting market dynamics.

Sikkim has a great wealth of natural and cultural attractions and really does not need large investment in hotel construction. Adventure/trekking travel is growing very fast and there is a need to link with environmental awareness among both visitors and host community, with the need to maintain cultural traditions, and the benefits derived from tourism should act as incentives to promote conservation practices and mitigate environmental degradation. Tour operators play a key role in the development of tourism industry with wide coverage in television, besides press and consumer magazine. For better marketing, tour operators should attend some of the important travel marts in Asia and Europe to be able to make contact with foreign agents to generate future business.

Sikkim has a great wealth of natural and cultural attractions and really does not need large investment in hotel construction. Adventure/trekking travel is growing very fast and there is a need to link with environmental awareness among both visitors and local community, with the need to maintain cultural traditions, and the benefits derived from tourism should act as an incentives to promote conservation practices and mitigate environmental degradation. Travel agents play a key role in the development of travel industry with wide coverage in television, besides press and consumer magazine.

Some of the relevant marketing problems faced by 'sensitive' and 'contributory' providers of ecotourism products, associated with the financial constraints that they face are: (i) positioning product in the tourism market; (ii) maintaining real time inventories/booking information especially when the office is not staffed; (iii) proving wider access to general information on products; and (iv) operating with a relatively small marketing budget.

3.4.3. Research

Research is urgently needed into psychographic and more meaningful profiles of tourists as a whole, not specially 'ecotourists', partly for marketing purposes but also to enable the industry to provide the kinds of experiences and services that people demand. Most of the data collected by Tourism Department relates to demographics, places visited, general expenditure and activities undertaken. The surveys typically do not ask about what people would like to experience while on tour and whether their expectations have been fulfilled after the tours. This problem has been recognized. The Tourism Department, for example, will be including new questions in its survey designed to elicit this kind of information (Preece and Oosterzee, 2007, in htpp:// www.environment.gov.au).

3.4.4. Education and Training

Education is a crucial ingredient in strategies for integrating biodiversity conservation and ecotourism. One of the most obvious deficiencies at present is the level of education and communication skills of ecotourism operators. Customers, tour operators, and local guides all need to be educated about proper behavior and practices in environmentally and culturally sensitive areas. The range of expertise varies enormously. Misinformation on biodiversity, ecology and management is common in the industry. This often has a detrimental effect on the tourism trade since many of the tourists traveling on ecotours are well-educated and may be alienated by deficient information and commentary. The education of tourists should begin with pre-departure information which familiarizes visitors with the specific problems and concerns of their destination. Tour operators and guides must be particularly aware of and sensitive to the areas they promote because they develop the itineraries and are responsible for their clients. Programmes of professional training and updating are needed, for travel agents, tour operators and field staffs to counter this problem. Some of the key areas that need to be addressed include: (i) the meaning of biodiversity and biodiversity conservation; (ii) the relationships between tourism and natural areas; (iii) ecology, wildlife studies and land management; (iv) ecological sustainability; (v) impacts of tourism and ways of preventing or minimizing them; (vi) interpretation of natural history; and (vii) ecosystem theory and practice.

Chapter 4

ECONOMIC VALUATION

4.1. INTRODUCTION

Ecological economics is only a 15-20 years old discipline. It sees the economy as a sub-system of environment or a larger natural ecosystem that is of a limited nature (Daly, 1999). This stand point is contrary to that of neoclassical economics according to which, economy is the total system, and nature is merely one of its sectors. According to this view, the ecosystem sector is required only for extracting resources and disposal of waste. Neoclassical economics stresses that the economy is whole, therefore, "the growth of economy is at the expense of nothing" (Daly, 1999); there is nothing like uneconomic growth. Ecological economics emphasizes that economic growth occurs as a result of the transformation of natural capital (environment and resources) into man-made capital. This transformation occurs within a "total environment", which is finite in several ways (Singh, et al., 2006).

Valuation of ecosystem services depends on several factors such as the size of territories and human population which receive them, and cultural traits of societies. Economic valuations have proved to be important tools in improving natural resources management and conservation. Much of the world's precious natural resources lie in the developing countries, it is ironical that few economic valuation have been done in these parts of the world. The case of Himalaya is no different. The usefulness of economic valuations with respect to the conservation and management of natural resources has been well documented in the literature (Pearce, et al. 1994).

When the market for a certain good is competitive enough, economic activities can be studied by the market pricing mechanism. Because this is usually not feasible in case of environmental goods with embodied natural and cultural heritage, particularly methods for economic valuation of such goods have to be applied (Verbic and Slabe-Erker, 2009). Economic valuations of natural resources have been used in conservation and management of protected areas (Pearce et al. 1994; Wilson and Carpenter, 1999). Contingent valuation method is widely applied in estimating the economic valuation of both marketed and non-marketed goods (Brookshire et al. 1983; Majid et al. 1983; Walsh et al. 1986; Dixon and Sherman, 1990).

Local communities often find themselves in a position where they have to decide on what spatial changes and development guidelines to implement within the scope of nationally or regionally adopted spatial and development planning documents. Their decisions must address not only operating costs, but also the positive and negative spatial impact of the development programmes on people's welfare. Ensuring that spatial and environmental impacts are given appropriate weight in the decision-making process, it is imperative to determine their monetary value (Verbic and Slabe-Erker, 2009).

In the case analyzed in this chapter, the impact of tourism and other developmental activities in Khangchendzonga Biosphere Reserves evaluated, together with its natural and cultural goods. This is an area with distinct qualities of international importance. The purpose of the study was to evaluate the overall value of environmental goods, i.e. the use value and the non-use value for residents and visitors to the area. For this purpose, the contingent valuation method was selected; mainly due to significant non-use values in the area, the total value for residents and visitors, and the varying selection of goods in this area. The contingent valuation method uses to estimate the willingness-to-pay for the protection and conservation of protected areas. Only stated preference methods, such as contingent valuation method (Whittington, 1998; Garrod and Willis, 1999; Nunes et al. 2003; Verbic, 2006) can be used to estimate environmental values such as biotic diversity, preservation of cultural and art collections, artefacts and monuments etc.

Contingent valuation surveys were first proposed in theory by Ciriacy-Wantrup (1947) as a method for eliciting market valuation of a non-market good. The first practical application of the technique was done by Davis (1963) on the economic value of recreation in the Maine woods. Numerous applications of the method to various public goods and studies of its methodological properties were conducted worldwide in the 1970s and 1980s. A review of the theoretical and empirical basis of contingent valuation is presented in Mitchell and Carson (1989), Arrow et al. (1993) and, more recently, in Moons (2003), Venkatachalam (2004) and Schlapfer (2006). Nowadays, the method is widely used in cost-benefit analysis and environmental impact assessment. Recent applications that are relevant for the present study include Hadker et al. (1997), Cicia and Scarpa (2000), Maharana et al. (2000), Lette and de Boo (2002), Navrud and Ready (2002), Laitila and Paulrud (2006), Bateman et al. (2006), Verbic and Slabe-Erker (2009) and Tadesse (2009).

A few studies have estimated the economic values of either tourism in specific protected areas, or ecotourism, let alone the overall economic value of protected areas around the world. This is because of data on ecotourism are not collected systematically by the private sector, governments, or the UN-WTO. This in turn is attributable to the fact that ecotourism is a relatively recent phenomena. In short, ecotourism and wildlife related tourism is big business. It was estimated, for instance, that in 1988 there were between 157 and 236 million international ecotourists worldwide. It was also estimated that between 79 and 157 million people could be considered wildlife oriented (Ceballos-Lascurain, 1996). If the above estimators and multipliers were applied to the UN-WTO data, the results suggested that ecotourism contributed between US$ 93 and 233 billion to the national income of various countries. It was further estimated that wildlife oriented tourism generated revenue ranged from US$ 47 to US$155 billion. More specifically, bird related tourism may have attracted as many as 78 million travelers with economic impacts as high as US$78 billion for the economies of the countries they visited (Filion et al. 1992).

The main concept of the contingent valuation method is to model individuals' responses in terms of their reactions in specific hypothetical situations (Verbic and Slabe-Erker, 2009). In the case of environmental evaluation, questions relate to the highest sum that individuals are prepared to pay for a change (conservation) at the environmental goods level (willingness-to-pay). Changes in the level of environmental goods can then be described by a number of different development scenarios. The form of the contingent valuation method was defined on the basis of scenarios and research objectives. This chapter describes the combine classical contingent valuation method with a closed-version of discrete choice method, where the protest responses are removed. The present analysis represents one of the relatively few applications of the method to the Biodiversity rich hot spot of the world, and certainly one of the very few applications of the method to Himalaya in general.

4.2. VALUE OF ECOSYSTEM SERVICES AND NATURAL CAPITAL AT A GLOBAL LEVEL

The Millennium Ecosystem Assessment Report (MEA 2005a and MEA 2005b) recognizes four categories of ecosystem services, viz., (i) provisioning services (goods such as food and freshwater); (ii) regulating services, e.g., disease control and climate regulation; (iii) cultural services, e.g., education and recreation; and (iv) supporting services, such as nutrient cycling and primary production. We all are familiar with goods derived from natural ecosystems, such as fodder from grasslands, food from oceans, fuelwood and timber from forests and pharmaceutical products from medicinal plants. In a broad sense, the benefits that come to humans from natural processes can be called ecosystem services (Singh et al. 2006). We can define ecosystem services as services which are generated as a result of interaction and exchange between biotic and abiotic components of ecosystems (Singh et al. 2006).

Recently, Costanza et al. (1997) made an estimate of the value of the world's ecosystem services and natural capital, which contribute to human welfare. They estimated the economic values of 17 ecosystem services for 16 major biome types, such as major forest types, estuaries, marine and freshwater based biomes (Table 4.1 and 4.2).

Table 4.1. Total annual value of ecosystem services of major ecosystem types

Ecosystem Type	Value Per Unit Area (US$ ha^{-1})	Total (Rate × Area) (Trillion US$)
Aquatic		
Open ocean	252	8.38
Coastal marine	4052	12.57
Wetland	14785	4.88
Lakes and rivers	8498	1.70
Total	27587	27.53
Terrestrial-natural and semi-natural		
Forest	969	4.71
Grassland	232	0.91
Total	1201	5.62
Manmade/intensely managed		
Cropland	92	0.13
Urban	0	0
Total	92	0.13
Grand Total	28880	33.28

Source: Costanza et al., 1997

Table 4.2. Total annual value of ecosystem services which include regulation of climate and gases, hazard protection, water regulation, erosion control, nutrient cycling, waste treatment, biological control, resource production and recreation/culture

Ecosystem Services	Value in Trillion US$
Soil formation	17.10
Recreation	3.00
Nutrient cycling	2.30
Water regulation and supply	2.03
Climatic regulation	1.80
Habitat	1.40
Flood and storm protection	1.10
Food and raw materials production	0.80
Genetic resources	0.80
Atmospheric gas balance	0.70
Pollination	0.40
Others	1.60
Total Value	33.03

Source: Costanza et al., 1997

For the entire world, the estimated value was in the range of US$ 16-54 trillion annually, with an average of US$ 33 trillion yr^{-1}, which is about twice as much as the global gross national product, US$ 18 trillion yr^{-1}. Costanza et al. (1997) acknowledge that their estimate represents first approximation, and is a minimum value, which is likely to increase with improvement in valuation techniques and as ecosystem services become depleted and scarce in the future. The immediate practical use of the estimates of ecosystem services is to help modify existing accounting at regional and national level to better reflect values of ecosystem services and natural capital.

4.3. ECONOMIC VALUATION OF ENVIRONMENT AND ECOSYSTEM SERVICES

The economic valuation of natural ecosystems is very limited in developing countries, although there are a number of studies on the topic, majority of them have been carried out in developed countries. It is being increasingly recognized now that there is a scope for market based approaches to environmental regulation, largely because of the worldwide adoption of market philosophy and development of suitable market mechanisms (Garrot and Willis, 1999). A number of techniques have been developed to value environmental goods and services. The environmental valuation techniques which are based on demand curves are generally divisible into two broad categories: (i) revealed preference methods; and (ii) stated preference methods.

The revealed preference methods depend on finding out actual purchase of goods which are related to environmental goods for which demand is to be determined. In stated preference methods the demand for environmental goods is not measured on the basis of actual purchase in the market place, but by examining individual's stated preference for environmental goods relative to their demands for other goods and services. Expressed preference techniques (EPT) depend on asking individuals explicitly how much they value environmental goods and services. In this, there is no requirement of complementary good (travel or house location) or a substitute good (compensating wage rate) to derive a demand curve. The two basic types of EPT's are: contingent valuation method (CVM) and sated preference (SP) or choice experiment techniques.

Several methods are available to evaluate recreational value of natural ecosystem. But in this study, contingent valuation method (CVM) was used. This method has been recommended as providing acceptable economic measures of the social benefits of recreational activities for both used and non-used values (Walsh, 1986; Navrud, 1992; Cordell and Bergstrom, 1993). The other method used in this type of assessment is cost-benefit analysis (Ableson, 1979; Kneese, 1984; Haneley and Spash, 1993) but it has a long controversial history (Hufschmidt et al. 1983).

Non-market valuation techniques can provide useful information for economic evaluation of national parks, and the results of such valuation can be incorporated more fully in benefit-cost analysis including conservation components to determine their viability (Munasinghe, 1993). In developing countries like India, the economic valuations of natural ecosystems are very few. Murthy and Menkhuas (1994) first time conducted a study on the economic aspects of wildlife protection in Keolado National Park, Bharatpur, Rajasthan, while Manoharan (1996) in Periyar Tiger Reserves of Kerala and Hadker et al. (1997) in Borvali National Park of Maharastra.

4.3.1. The Contingent Valuation Method (CVM)

The contingent valuation method (CVM) attempts to value non-market goods by asking people directly for their willingness-to-pay to obtain specified improvements or to avoid decrements in them, using social scientific survey techniques (Heberlein, 1988; Bishop and Heberlein, 1992; Arrow et al. 1993). The CVM uses a questionnaire or survey to create a hypothetical market or referendum, and then allows the respondent to use it to state or reveal his or her WTP for recreation, option, existence and bequest values (Mitchell and Carson, 1989; Mullarkey and Bishop, 1995). The main concern in using the WTP technique was with the validity of responses, specifically, would the respondents actually pay the money they agreed to pay in survey?

The Contingent Valuation Method remains the subject of heated debate within the non-market valuation literature due to hypothetical nature of markets (Hanemann, 1994), and its susceptibility to biases (Cummings et al. 1986; Mitchell and Carson, 1989; Freeman, 1993). Attempts have been made to minimize the biases in order to get a reliable estimate of economic value of recreation. One of the most important potential biases of CVM is scenario misspecification, especially on the amenity to be valued. This is a serious bias in estimating non-use values. In the present study, the bias should have been minimal for use values. Response was taken only when visitors were familiar with the non-use goods after visiting the park. In person interviews were initiated by informing respondents about the work and background of the Khangchendzonga Biosphere Reserves. Respondents were told about the nature of the work. The nature of the interview was explained, and the issue of the park was introduced. Face-to-face interviews secure a high response rate as to other survey techniques. In CV exercise, interviewer adopted a double bounded dichotomous choice formulation, as it is more information intensive (Hanemann et al. 1991). First, the respondents were asked whether they were willing to pay for the non-market commodity benefits after being given proper information about the commodity. If the answer was "No", the process ended there with that particular respondent. If the answer was "Yes", then the second step was to determine the maximum amount he/she was willing to pay. The maximum willingness to pay was determined by bidding process. The interviewer started the bidding by a particular amount. If it was above his/her willingness to pay, the interviewer reduced the bid gradually until the answer was "Yes" and the value was recorded. If the respondent agreed to the interviewer's initial bidding amount, the interviewer gradually raised the bid until the respondent said "No". Respondents who showed inability to pay in cash were considered for willingness to actually do service in the park (Maharana, 2000; Maharana, et al. 2000; Tadesse, 2009).

Socio-economic details were also collected for regression purposes. Apart from name and addresses, information on age, sex, education, occupation, and income were also collected. An attempt was also made to establish the importance of environmental issues perceived by the respondents, and to measure whether or not the respondent demonstrated implicit value for the environment and non-use values. The question regarding the environmental attitudes of the respondents e.g., how they will give rank for the justification of biodiversity loss, and it avoidance and reasons for visiting to Khangchendzonag Biosphere Reserves were also analyzed. These preferences were measured on a five-point scale ranging from "Strongly Agreed", "Agreed", "Neutral", "Disagreed", to "Strongly disagreed".

4.4. AN ANALYSIS OF THE WILLINGNESS-TO-PAY (WTP)

4.4.1. Socio-Economic Analysis

Prior to starting the analysis of willingness-to-pay, Table 4.3 gives descriptive statistics of the key variables used in the regression estimation. Name and address, age, education, occupation and annual income were collected from the interviewees. The preliminary findings and summary statistics of the sample of 545 respondents are presented. In the case of local community members the sample had a mean age of 36 years, with respondents ranging from 20 to 55 years of age. More than 90% of the sample consisted of male respondents. The mean household size was 5 members and ranged from 2 to 9 members. As for as domestic visitors were concerned, mean age was 33 with respondents ranging from 19 to 65 years of age. The foreign visitors mean age was 39, ranging from 20 to 67 years of age (Table 4.3). With respect to educational qualification of the local communities, 15% of the respondents were illiterate and 23% had less than 10 years of schooling. About 34% of the respondents had obtained high school, 9% higher secondary and 19% had a bachelor's degree. The educational qualification of the domestic visitors showed that 9% were master degree holders, 81% bachelor degree holders and 10% had higher secondary education. In the case of foreign visitors, 25% of respondents had master degree, 60% bachelor degrees and 15% had a higher secondary education.

Occupation of local community members showed 31% of respondents from service sector, 32% farming and off-farm activities, 21% tourism and 16% business people. Occupation of domestic and foreign tourists showed 45% and

40% in government service, 34% and 51% professionals, 10% and 6% business, 10% and 1% students, respectively. Small fractions (1 to 2%) of domestic and foreign visitors were retired persons. About thirty four per cent of the foreign tourists were French and Swedish, 16% British, 11% German, 5% American and 33% were from other countries.

Table 4.3. Descriptive statistics of key variables

Respondents	Variables					
	Age	Sex	EDQ	OCU	INC ($)	WTP ($)
Foreign Visitors						
Mean	38.96	1.41	15.11	4.25	4011	8.84
Std. Dev	11.73	0.49	1.50	0.82	4281	11.94
Domestic Visitors						
Mean	32.71	1.18	14.90	4.01	159	1.91
Std. Dev	8.29	0.38	1.12	1.23	66	4.05
Local Community						
Mean	36.20	1.09	8.53	3.19	832	6.20
Std. Dev	8.67	0.29	4.76	1.42	375	19.08

AGE: Respondent's age in years; SEX: Male-1, Female-2; EDQ: Year of schooling; INC: Income (households annual income for local community and monthly for visitors); OCU: Occupation; Service- 5, Professional-4, Bussiness-3, Retaired-2 and Student-1 for visitors and Tourism involved-5, Service-4, Bussiness-3, Labourer-2, and Agriculture-1 for local community members; WTP: Willingness-to-pay (per trip for visitors and annually for local community).

Source: Maharana et al. 2000

The attractions of visitors were diverse. A majority came for recreation/trekking, followed by wilderness and bird watching. Analysis of visitors' attitude on environment perception towards protection of the Khangchendzonga Biosphere Reserves revealed that 42% and 59% of domestic and foreign visitors considered it "Very Important", 38% and 32% "Important", 12% and 5% "Not Very Important", and 8% and 4% "Unimportant", respectively (Maharana, 2000). Perception on biodiversity loss justification in the context of India showed that the majority of both domestic and foreign tourist agreed to this point. A question on direct relevance of the Khangchendzonga Biosphere

Reserves for avoidance of biodiversity loss at any cost was not acceptable to the local community, the reason being their dependency on natural resources. In contrast, about 50% of both domestic and foreign tourists agreed to the avoidance of biodiversity loss at any cost (Table 4.4).

Table 4.4. Respondent's perception on the importance of environmental issues (%)

Opinion	Respondents	QUESTIONS	
		Biodiversity loss justification in the context of India*	Avoidance of KBR biodiversity loss at any cost
Strongly disagreed	LC	-	28
	DT	3	2
	IT	1	2
Disagreed	LC	-	40
	DT	4	24
	IT	1	28
Neutral	LC	-	17
	DT	19	19
	IT	22	13
Agreed	LC	-	13
	DT	64	48
	IT	63	50
Strongly agreed	LC	-	2
	DT	10	7
	IT	13	7

LC=local community; DT= domestic tourists; IT= foreign tourists; * this question was not asked to the local community
Source: Maharana et al. 2000

In response to environmental problems and steps to be taken for conservation, about 10% said that there was no need to conserve the biodiversity of the biosphere because it was already in good condition, while 90% expressed conservation needs (Maharana, 2000). On the question about who should conserve and maintain the Biosphere, about 55% were not sure. Of proposed implementing authorities, the majority of international tourists felt that the conservation in the biosphere should be collective effort, with the next ranked being government and community jointly. The domestic tourists responded similarly, desiring government and community jointly to play the main role, followed by collective effort and then government (Table 4.5). When asked whether they feel responsible for the maintenance of the Trail route, 85% of the respondents gave a positive response, whereas 15% responded negatively.

Table 4.5. Respondents attitude for the protection of biosphere reserve

Implementing authority	Visitors			
	International		Domestic	
	Number	(%)	Number	(%)
Government	38	12	19	15
Non-government organization (NGO)	10	3	9	7
Local community	10	3	12	10
Government and Community	123	38	49	39
Collective effort*	142	43	30	24
Can't say	2	1	6	5

Includes visitors, local community, travel operators, NGOs, and government
Source: Maharana et al. 2000

4.4.2. Analyzing Stated Willingness-to-Pay (WTP)

Generally those respondents who are getting direct benefits from the park were considered for analysis of WTP, but in the present study the WPT was assumed to be a function of the respondents' personal characteristics and income level. Another variable, education level, was used as an explanatory variable. Greater number of years of schooling would arguably increase the knowledge of a person. Perhaps education would help a person comprehend news about the environmental effects of economic development. Age and gender were also used as explanatory variables. Results of this study for willingness-to-pay are presented in Table 4.6.

The result shows that the average response rate was 45% on the question regarding the motivation behind the respondents WTP for conservation. Only 31 local households indicated a willingness to pay for better management of the KBR. About 25 households said that they were willing to pay, but due to their financial constraints and other responsibilities they were unable to pay.

**Table 4.6. Results from the contingent valuation (CV) question
(Maharana et al. 2000)**

Variables	WTP		
	Foreign visitors	Domestic visitors	Local community
Mean value per visitor (US$)	8.84	1.91	6.20
**Aggregate value for all visitors (US$)	5852	1226	1699
*Respondent with WTP (%)	50	40	33
+ Response rate (%)	49	19	35

WTP: Willingness to pay; US$ 1= Rs. 38/- (as per the conversion rate in 1997).
** The non-respondents were assumed to have a WTP equal to those that answered.
*Based on total respondents who responded positively for WTP.
+ Based on total visitors/households.

Thirty households indicated willingness to perform voluntary work by providing manual labour for trail maintenance and cleanup. Respondents who were willing to volunteer agreed to set aside about one day per month. Some of them said they could provide seedlings for plantations in the surrounding areas. Nine households refused completely to pay in kind or in cash for conservation. In case of foreign tourists, only 49% indicated a positive reaction to WTP for conservation, while 27% agreed on condition that the amount would be utilized in a constructive manner, and 24% refused to pay. In case of domestic tourists, about 60% respondents showed an indifferent attitude towards paying for conservation because they felt that it was the responsibility of the state government and local communities.

An analysis of WTP provides an opportunity to study the content and context validity of the interview schedule. An Ordinary Least Square (OLS) regression was used to analyses WTP. The regression revealed that the variables attained the expected signs, as presented in Table 4.7. The R^2 value is encouraging in the present context. Age showed a positive correlation with WTP in the case of all domestic, foreign visitors and local communities. It was found that the middle age group and older age group of people could spare the money to accept CV bids while the young age group could spare less. This suggests that age is a major factor for all types of respondents to accept the WTP.

Educational qualification did not show a significant correlation with WTP when zero bid was included, however, on exclusion of "refuse the bids", it showed positive correlation with WTP ($P<0.003$). This was mainly attributed to less educated respondents opting for most of the "refused the bids" for WTP. About 55% of the total responses were 'refused to pay". Occupation was not a major factor to accept the CV bids. Those people who were directly involved with tourism related activities and getting more economic returns were interested to pay for WTP as compared to those who were not getting the economic benefits from tourism. Our results also indicate that businessmen were willing to pay more than professionals. This finding has important policy implications as businessmen have the most potential for financing environmental improvements. Sex also did not influence the visitation rate and WTP for conservation. The income of visitors significantly influenced their WTP for conservation of the area (Table 4.7).

For the entire samples, using means of variables, the estimated willingness-to-pay for the management of KBR was USD 8.84 by foreign visitors per trip, US$ 1.91 by domestic visitors per trip, and US$ 6.20 by the local community on an annual basis. This shows that the foreign visitors had higher recreational/ conservation values than did the domestic visitors and local community members. The question regarding the confidentiality concerning the right amount for their conservation contribution, about 26% of local community members, 22% of domestic and 20% of foreign visitors stated that they were "very confident", while 55%, 52%, and 40% were "confident", respectively. About 13% of local community members, 16% of domestic, and 28% of foreign visitors were "undecided", remaining were "not very confident" (Table 4.7). These responses suggest that the amount stated by the respondents were valid.

Table 4.7. Result of multiple regression estimation (Maharana et al. 2000)

Component				
Dependent variables		WTP		
No. of observation		243		
Multiple R		0.348		
Squared multiple R		0.121		
Adjusted Squared Multiple R		0.103		
Standard Error		489.155		
Variables	Coefficient	Std. Error	t value	P<
AGE	9.534	2.860	3.334	0.001
SEX	-41.927	68.196	-0.615	0.539
EDQ	34.167	11.195	3.052	0.003
OCU	-6.886	31.567	-0.218	0.828
INC	0.005	0.002	3.148	0.002
Analysis of variance				
	Sum-of-squares	DF	Mean-Squares	F-Ratio	P<
Regression	7828703.690	5	1565740.738	6.544	0.000
Residual	5.67075E+03	237	239272.254		

AGE: Age, SEX: Sex, EDQ: Educational qualification, OCU: Occupation, INC: Income.

The number of visitors is increasing at a very fast rate in Sikkim Himalaya. The rate increased from 155% from 1980 to 1995 (Rai and Sundriyal, 1997). Compare to other parks in Sikkim, the frequency of visitors was less in KBR because most of the visitors seldom return to trek for a second time in the same area. Therefore, the WTP stated by all the visitors was for that particular period. The demand for recreation in Sikkim Himalaya by foreign visitors was price elastic. This observation is consistent with previous recreational studies (Navrud and Mungatana, 1994). Walsh (1986) gave an overview of the price elasticities of demand for various recreational activities. There were 23 cases of outdoor recreation activities with a price elasticity of demand. The price elasticity of demand for a recreational activity is generally low when the proportion of income spent on it is low (Walsh, 1986). Income elasticity in studies done in developed countries is small, but much larger than that observed in present study. This may be an indication of the income effects at the national income level. As our income levels grow the income elasticity may improve for environmental goods. The probability of participation increased with age and increasing income. The magnitude of economic problems restricted domestic visitors from visiting the reserve because the entry fees for the reserve are relatively high as compared to other protected areas. Therefore, visits to the KBR are given low priority by most of the domestic tourists, that is, except for a few rich individuals and people from India's West Bengal, Maharastra, Delhi and Gujrat states. The findings of this study are similar to Walsh (1986), where age and income appeared to be the most important socio-economic variable determining the probability of participation in recreation activity. This was expected, as an increase in income level would show respondents' greater willingness to spend on recreation. Every one-year increase in education increased the WTP by 5% (Hadker et al.1997). Attitudes are good predictors of a person's actual and sated behaviour.

As already mentioned, there are relatively few applications of contingent valuation to national parks available for comparison. However, as can be inferred from the application of contingent valuation to a cross-border region. Compared to other parts of India, the frequency of visitors was less in KBR, because most of the visitors seldom return to trek for a second time in the same area. Therefore, the WTP stated by all the visitors was for that particular visit. This study revealed that the visitors' WTP did not depend upon the benefits they would get in preserving the biosphere, but most of them stated that their WTP was just to keep the beautiful, unexploited landscape and rich biodiversity of this area intact. Same observation was also reported by Tadesse (2009). The demand for nature/ecotourism in Sikkim by international visitors has also been increasing.

The analysis of qualitative landscape features showed that Sikkim was increasingly interested in the conservation of historical and traditional flora and fauna. Thus compare this result with those from available contingent valuation studies in the national park. Fomenko *et al.,* (1997) performed an economic valuation of park Gorushka in the Yaroslavi oblast of Russia, and established that the average combined (in money and in kind) WTP for residents was USD 2.3 per year. Kluvankova (1999) analyzed MalaFatraNational Park in the SlovakRepublic, and established that the average WTP was USD 86 and USD 4 respectively for residents and visitors. Hadker *et al.,* (1997) performed willingness-to-pay for Borivali national park of India and established that the average WTP for residents was Rs 21 per year. Tadesse (2009) analyzed SMNP of Ethiopia, and established that the average WTP for foreign visitors were USD 8.83.

The economic valuation of the KBR, which is an important Indian Himalayan biosphere reserve with internationally recognized qualities, by the use of classical contingent valuation method. Within this framework an econometric analysis of willingness-to-pay has performed. It demonstrates that the contingent valuation method (WTP) is a promising approach since it includes a broad range of societal concerns about reserve/park management. However, the WTP lacks inclusion of non-monetary contributions. The WTP for the KBR is encouraging and showed positive attitude. Value of willingness-to-pay was positively affected by the respondent's income, age, and education, his perception of probable damage to the area, his perception of natural and cultural heritage in general and the number of values embodied in the area's environmental goods. At last, the average individual value of willingness-to-pay was used in order to calculate the aggregate willingness-to-pay. The aggregate value obtained seems to provide a relatively good reflection of international visitors' perception of use value, and above all the non-use value of the KBR. It is especially important to note that the local communities are willing-to-pay for environmental management, mostly in kind or time for services. Therefore, CVM could be a useful tool in providing more relevant information for decision-makers for investment and policy purposes in biodiversity hot spot and protected area management. The present analysis represents one of the very few applications of the method to Himalayan region.

Although the economic valuation of cultural goods and services has gained increasing interest from policy makers and cultural economists, few studies have been ·undertaken to place an economic value on cultural heritage sites and biosphere reserves, despite the debate over their value to society and their level of government funding and support.

Chapter 5

PARTICIPATORY ECOTOURISM PLANNING AND BIODIVERSITY CONSERVATION

5.1. INTRODUCTION

Hindu-Kush Himalayan region is a site of high biodiversity value, and one that is facing growing threats from a variety of sources including commercial logging, farming practices and tourism. As concern grows over the loss of both natural and cultural heritage in this region, attention is turning to strategies, which seek to link conservation with tourism development and generate incentives to conserve the resources on which economic benefits depend (Maharana, 2000). The economic significance of tourism industry is multifarious. Tourism development has a great deal of appeal for its role in the economic development of inaccessible mountain area and its impact on local society, economy and the environment. The most important economic benefits of tourism are the earnings of convertible foreign exchange (Malhotra, 1998). But the criticism of tourism parallels a general paradigm shift away from purely growth-oriented economic development towards more sustainable forms of development (Friedmann et al. 1980; Redclift, 1987; Brookfield, 1988). The new paradigm requires programmes that limit the negative effects of economic behaviour on local environments and cultures. It proposes linkages between economy, culture and ecology in what Norgaard (1984) calls "Co-evolutionary development" and what others have termed "eco-development" (Farvar and Glaeser, 1979). Brockelman (1988) and Mckean (1989) view tourism as a way to foster meaningful cross-cultural relationships as well as to promote environmental conservation and more equitable distribution of tourism earnings.

All conservation efforts must involve the participation of the local people based on their interest and skills under the program that offer them social and economic benefits. Innovative programs of this kind have been developed world wide in and around national parks and biosphere reserves. The majority of population on the national parks still depends directly on the natural resources for some or other crucial elements of their survival. This is even true of protected areas than elsewhere, for the simple reason that highly ecosystem dependent people predominantly inhabit in the protected areas, (Kothari et al. 1989). Broadly community based conservation could be described as a conservation of biological diversity based on involvement of local communities in decision making.

As early in 1975, the IUCN passed a resolution on at its 12[th]General Assembly in Kinshasa, Zaire; recognize the value and importance of "traditional ways of life and the skill of the people which enable them to live in harmony with their environment". The resolution recommended that the governments should maintain and encourage traditional methods of living and devise means by which indigenous people may bring their lands into conservation areas with out relinquishing their ownership, use or tenure rights. Public support for conservation therefore becomes a necessity. Indeed, local people because of their day-to-day interaction and depends on these areas are often at the forefront of protest against the degradation caused by outside commercial interests (Tadese, 2009).

Conservationists in the recent years view local people support to the protected areas management as an important element of biodiversity conservation. This is often linked to the direct benefits, which the local communities get from the protected areas. Establishment of protected areas (PAs) has been the most widely accepted means of biodiversity conservation so far, supported by National and International agencies. Local communities are vulnerable to the establishment of parks, particularly in developing countries since their livelihoods are dependent on them (Rodger, 1989). In the recent years it is being increasingly recognized that parks should play a role in sustaining local people livelihoods (McNeely, 1993). This falls very much in the context of the discussion on Convention on Biological Diversity (CBD's) goals of conservation and sustainable use of biological diversity. Several projects linking conservation and development have been promoted around parks. In general the involvement of the community on biological diversity conservation is vital for the long sustainability of the protected areas and the national parks.

As part of strategy of biodiversity conservation, increase stakeholder participation in tourism and natural resource conservation through activities in the investigated areas. The hypothesis is that if income generation is dependent on the continued availability of biodiversity, then those entrepreneurs and stakeholders will have to act upon economic incentives to conserve the resources (protected areas and other natural resources) on which income depends.

5.2. TOURISM AND DEVELOPMENT OF LOCAL AND REGIONAL ECONOMY

Tourism is a multifaceted economic asset. It is a smokeless industry and is a representation of a cross section of the whole economy. As such it is an effective tool of economic growth as far as the tourist places are concerned. Thus tourism attractions are distinct and unique economic resources. In KBR, most of the tourism earnings come from organized pack tour. Some local people work exclusively for Himalayan Mountaineering Institute (HMI) training courses as pack animal porters. Employment in trekking and mountaineering is seasonal. Most porters, pack-animal operators and cooks work not more than four to five months a year, but most men are employed on a long-standing basis by Gangtok based tour operator. The same situation is also prevalent in the Nepal Himalaya (Adams, 1992).

Yuksam people started their tourism business in 1960s, and by the 2008 about 70% of all households engaged in tourism related business. Lodges have become an increasingly important part of the regional economy. An immensely popular investment in tourism since 1990s is purchasing and keeping packstock for trekking and mountaineering courses. The multiplier effects of the cash earned in tourism have both increased non-tourism employment and enlarged the market for local agricultural products.

5.2.1. Government Investments

In ninth five year plan of the Sikkim Government had allocated Rs. 40 million to the tourism sector. However, with the ushering in of the present regime in 1995, a greater focus on tourism has been witnessed. A specific tourism Master Plan for five years were developed and implemented with an anticipated budget of over Rs. 30 crores to develop tourism industry as a sustainable economic activity. The Central government allotted Rs. 20 million and State government Rs. 12 million for infrastructure development, promotion and refurbishment of monasteries and heritage sites (Anonymous, 1997).

The investment in key infrastructure development by the state government was Rs. 41715000 in 1998-99. The thrust of the state investments means to foster and develop tourism in the state. Out of the total investments, major portion (50%) for accommodation and transport services, followed by 12% in advertisements, 5% in event organizations, 3% each in printing and public relations and 30% for other purposes (Anonymous, 1997).

5.3. COMPONENTS OF ECOTOURISM AND CONSERVATION

Three key areas that link conservation with ecotourism enterprises are focused in the analysis. As the main focus is biodiversity conservation, there is a need to increase stakeholder participation in tourism development and natural resource conservation through activities in the following areas.

5.3.1. Increasing Community and Private Sector Biodiversity Conservation Initiatives

Activities include:

(i) Community ecotourism plans covering site–enhancement, and trail and site maintenance.
(ii) Natural resource management and monitoring and conservation education.
(iii) Supporting fuelwood reduction measures by tour operators and local lodges.
(iv) Supporting local NGOs working in ecotourism and conservation.

5.3.2. Increasing Economic Returns from Community-Based Ecotourism

Activities include:

(i) Training in ecotourism services, e.g. for guides, lodge-owners, cooks and porters.

(ii) Supporting new community ecotourism enterprises, i.e., vegetable growing, indigenous food promotion, fuelwood saving, equipment hire for treks.

(iii) Developing marketing strategies for community-based ecotourism and tour operators ecotourism activities.

(iv) Conducting market research and developing new ecotourism products, e.g. off-season activities, and indigenous food products.

5.3.3. Improving and Contributing to Policy-Making on Conservation and Ecotourism

Activities include:

(i) Scientific and participatory monitoring of tourism activities and impacts.

(ii) Sharing of research and monitoring findings among policy-makers, communities and the private sectors.

(iii) Promoting public-private sector dialogue through workshops, exchanges and policy review.

5.4. COMMUNITY ECOTOURISM PLANNING

Despite all the claims of good governance and sustainable management, it is clear that the tremendous growth of nature based tourism has not been matched by government efforts to adequately plan, implement and monitor developments through an administrative and legal mechanism. Community participation in the conservation of biological diversity is not that much common in the KBR due to the lack of knowledge about biodiversity conservation and ecotourism in protected areas and the biosphere reserves in general. Similar observations were also reported by Tadase (2009) in Semen Mountains National Park of Ethiopia.

A critical element of planning and subsequent actions in ecotourism is a focus on appreciative inquiry, finding and building upon positive attributes and values in local environments and groups of stakeholders. Unlike traditional rural development efforts that incorporate PLA techniques and focus on problem identification and solving, the approach taken in KBR asks: what is that you value in your community and environment? What excites you most about where you live? What is the most positive vision you have of your environment and community in the future? What do we need to do to get to you vision of the future? The focus is on finding the causes of success and motivation rather than failure as the basis for community planning.

The critical element of planning and subsequent actions in ecotourism is the focus upon positive attributes and values of local environment. Community members were asked to "Discover" the elements in their environment and community that represent the best of what they are and what they do. Positive attributes identified by community members are: (i) lots of greenery; (ii) community unity seen in actions to help others; (iii) meeting tourists from many different countries; (iv) fresh air; (v) dense forests; (vi) Yuksam is the first capital of Sikkim; (vii) historical importance of Yuksam.

Communities were then asked to "Dream" to think of what the best vision of Yuksam might be in 10 years time. What would you like to see in Yuksam 10 years from now: (i) more forest cover; (ii) more tourists in Yuksam; (iii) no litter in Yuksam and along the trails; (iv) more income from tourists.

A community based conservation approach to achieve the sustainable tourism is being tested in the KBR (Maharana, 2000). This programme can foster changes in local attitudes towards conservation and ultimately have the intended result. There are varieties of community participation in the conservation of biological diversity. According to (Pretty and Kothari, 1989), there are seven different types of participation of the community on biological diversity and the natural resources, i. e. (i) passive participation; (ii) participation in information giving; (iii) participation of consultation; (iv) participation of material incentives; (v) functional participation; (vi) interactive participation; and (vii) self mobilization. In addition to the activities identified by the local community, the Khangchendzonga Conservation Committee (local NGO) organized their own clean-up campaign of the major trekking route (Fig 5.1), generating an initial fund for further activities through the sale of bottle and tins collected during clean-up campaign (Table 5.1). In order to beautify the surrounding locality, indigenous fruit and flower-bearing species were sorted out and planted with the active participation of school children and the village community. The evaluation of these activities that were done annually reflected the pride taken by the local people and ensured their continuity.

The survey result of Semen Mountains National Park, Ethiopia also showed that the participation of the community in conservation related activities were low. The park managers and elder villagers of the SMNP in focus group discussion told that some community members participated in conservation practices like building of dams and construction of terraces, to prevent soil erosion, construction of road as well as the plantation of eucalyptus trees for the source of fuelwood in between 1992 to 1995.

Figure 5.1. Clean-up campaigns in Yuksam and its surrounding area along trail route.

Table 5.1. Participation of local communities in conservation related activities in the Khangchendzonga Biosphere Reserves (KBR) in Sikkim Himalaya

Activities	Yuksam-Dzongri-Goechha La trekking corridor		
	Male	Female	Total
Clean-up campaign	61	44	105
Tree palntation	104	43	147
Trail maintenance	28	11	39
Lake clean-up	7	3	10
Total	208	101	309

Source: Maharana, 2000

During the survey period (2007-2008), it was observed that from the total of 300 respondents, about 269 respondents, i e. (89.66%) were participated in conservation related activities like planting of eucalyptus trees for the purpose of fuelwood and construction materials, cleaning up campaign, trail maintenance, building of terraces to prevent the soil from erosion, guarding of the natural environment from any external damage and providing information and creating

awareness about the national park and its protection for other people residing in
the park area and have no knowledge about the importance of the SMNP and its
biological resources. From the total participated in conservation related activities
220 (81.78%) were males and 49 (18.22%) were females. Considering the activity
that the community participated in the conservation related activities the most
dominant was tree plantation which covered 33.46%. The remaining 31 (10.33%)
of households of different villages not participated in biological diversity
conservation of the national park. This may be due to lack of knowledge about
conservation and protection of biological resources and the physical environment
and it also may be due to lack of incentives that may motivate in the participation
of biological diversity conservation (Table 5.2).

The critical element of planning and subsequent actions in ecotourism is the
focus upon positive attributes and values of local environment. Yuksam and
Khecheopalri lake surrounding residents have readily accepted the principle of
local contributions to conservation activities and enthusiastically attended in
conservation related activities.

**Table 5.2. Participation of local community in conservation related activities
in SMNP, Ethiopia (2007-2008)**

Activities	Male		Female		Total	
	(No)	(%)	(No)	(%)	(No)	(%)
Tree plantation	68	25.28	22	8.18	90	33.46
Clean up campaign	50	18.59	12	4.46	62	23.05
Trail maintenance	30	11.15	-	-	30	11.15
Building of terraces	42	15.61	10	3.72	52	19.33
Guarding the natural environment	20	7.43	3	1.11	23	8.55
Providing information and creation of awareness	10	3.72	2	0.74	12	4.46
Total	220	81.78	49	18.22	269	100

Source: Tadesse (2009)

KCC (local NGO) has developed a Code of Conduct for visitors and tour operators to follow the ethics of conservation in the KBR (Table 5.3). The Code of Conduct was broadly divided into seven points. The compliance of code of conduct were measure in a five point scale ranging from "strongly agreed", "agreed", "neutral", "disagreed", and "strongly disagreed". Among all the issues it has been observed that 58% of the tour operator strongly agreed for complying properly the COC.

5.5. STRATEGIES FOR INTEGRATING BIODIVERSITY ISSUES IN PRODUCTION SECTORS

At the national level, integrating biodiversity issues in agriculture, fishery, and forestry management encourages sustainable harvesting and minimizing negative impact on biodiversity. Biodiversity will only be conserved and sustainably used when it becomes a main stream concern of production sectors. Agriculture is dependent on biodiversity, but agricultural practices in recent decades have focused on maximizing yields. Enterprise based vegetable production will be one of the key activities in this regard. Research and development have focused on few relatively productive species, thus ignoring the potential importance of agro-biodiversity.Effective response strategies include intensification, which minimizes the need for expanding total area for production, so allowing more area for biodiversity conservation. Practices such as integrated pest management, some forms of organic farming and protection of field margins, riparian zones, and other non-cultivated habitats with in farms can promote synergistic relationship between agriculture, domestic biodiversity, and wild biodiversity. However, assessment of biodiversity contributions from such management reveals little data about contributions to regional biodiversity conservation.

5.6. CONTRIBUTION OF THE PRIVATE SECTORS ON BIODIVERSITY CONSERVATION

The private sector can make significant contribution to biodiversity conservation. Some parts of the private sectors showing greater willingness-to-pay to biodiversity conservation. As part of the hypothesis to increase income from responsible tourism, the trade association of Sikkim and Travel Agent Association of Sikkim were encouraged to build links with an equivalent association in Nepal, The Trekking Agent Association of Nepal (TAAN). Lodge operators can also play a major role in biodiversity conservation in the area.

5.7. GOVERNANCE APPROACHES FOR THE PROMOTION OF BIODIVERSITY CONSERVATION

The sectoral approach of different departments was inadequate in addressing the management aspects in holistic manner. Government approaches to support biodiversity conservation and sustainable use of biological resources is required at all levels, with supportive laws and policies developed by central governments provide the security of tenure and authority essential for sustainable management at lower levels. The principle that biodiversity should be managed at the lowest appropriate level has led to decentralization in many parts of the world, with variable results. The key to success is strong institutions of all levels, with security of tenure and authority at the lower levels essential in providing incentives for sustainable management.

The various private sector stakeholders who were engaged in tourism operation had their own problems and expected incentives from the government. The local community, which is an internal component of tourism development, had a limited approach with the government, but this will be significantly strengthened. The local community based conservation group KCC has been empowered by various agencies to monitor and implement conservation activities. The State government has incorporated some of the policy issues in the master plan and established Tourism Development Corporation for better management of tourism sector.

Conservation requires a range of interventions, and while the enterprise approach will be a key component of future programs in Sikkim as well as entire Himalayan region, it will not necessarily be the only one. For entrepreneurs to undertake and continue conservation actions that support their livelihoods, it seems critical that they have some level of decision-making power over the resources in question. It appears that unless this is possible, economic benefits from an enterprise are unlikely to be effective as incentives to conserve. In Sikkim, there was little decision-making power over natural resources among the range of entrepreneurs, thus there would seem a little chance of economic incentives turning into actions to conserve biodiversity on which tourism depends. In Sikkim, the natural resources have for the most part been managed by the State

Government with permits and rights for subsistence extraction given by state departments. Little exists in the way community management of forests. But, by engaging stakeholders in a debate over the value of biodiversity in the State economy and the most efficient way this can be conserved, local stakeholder at the KBR are now participating in the on-going discussions over how biodiversity conservation can be conducted. The traditional decision-makers, such as government, are now increasingly highlighting the important role that local institutions can play. As the numbers of visitors (domestic and foreign) increases, the need to be proactive on promoting and supporting a responsible tourism ethic among consumers, suppliers, and producers alike is imperative. A number of activities have been identified and presented in Table 5.4. The players in sustainable development and management are tourists, tour operators, government, and the local communities are therefore called on to find new forms of coexistence and the right solutions for themselves for the survival of the industry. Sikkim has a great potential to increase its revenue through planned tourism if adopting policies suitable for tourism development.

As part of an approach to biodiversity conservation, ecotourism, defined as environmentally and socially responsible tourism, clearly has a role to play in Hindu-kush Himalayan region. As the number of visitors both domestic and international increase, the need to be proactive on promoting and supporting a responsible tourism ethic among consumers, suppliers and producers alike is imperative. There is a need to have collaboration between public and private sectors, as well as local communities, and a participatory design can produce results that contribute to conserving biodiversity assets that are of global significance.

On the Conservation Front

Conservation requires a range of interventions, and while the enterprise approach will be a key component of future programmes in Sikkim, it will not necessarily be the only one. For entrepreneurs to undertake and continue conservation actions that support their livelihoods, it seems critical that they have some level of decision-making power over the resources in question. It appears that unless this is possible, economic benefits from an enterprise are unlikely to be effective as incentives to conserve.

In Sikkim, there is little decision-making power over natural resources among the range of entrepreneurs, and thus there would seem a little chance of economic incentives turning into actions to conserve biodiversity on which tourism depends.

In Sikkim, the natural resources have for the most been managed by the State Government with permits and rights for subsistence extraction given by state departments. Little exists in the way of community management of forests. But by engaging stake-holders in a debate over the value of biodiversity in the state economy and the most efficient way it can be conserved, local stakeholders at the trail site are now participating in the on-going discussions over how biodiversity conservation can be conducted. Increasingly, traditional decision-makers, such as government, are highlighting the important role that local institutions can play.

In the case of Sikkim, the most important feature of the enterprise-based approach was to provide a framework in which to analyze and develop the potential of tourism for more than one type of stakeholder. Furthermore, it provided a means to argue that long-term benefits from tourism would only be possible if those whose income depended on the activity had a greater decision-making power in natural resource management.

5.8. SUGGESTIONS FOR IMPROVING THE PRESENT SITUATION

After making an inventory of various tourist attractions, their important features, historical, religious, social and cultural and scenic aspects, and discussing various other significant considerations of tourism and its related phenomenon. Its existing and potential resources, problems and prospects can be analyses for the overall planned development of tourism and also for the betterment and maintenance of the sites and heritage.

A number of potential suggestive measures for the management of tourism in KBR and Sikkim Himalaya as well is follows:

5.8.1. Physical Infrastructure

The necessary infrastructure for tourism development such as trails, communication, campsites and drinking water along Yuksan-Dzongri-Goechha La trail route is rudimentary and often lacking.

Trails

Trail conditions are variable with some well-engineered sections. However, at many other points trails are fair to poor. Two examples are the portion of the trail just before reaching to Tshoka and the trail approaching to Dzongri. Most of the trail conditions are substandard, very narrow and denuded as a result of trail erosion and landslide. There are many other precarious spots which inhibit easy access. Therefore, the first priority should be given to improving the trails and widening them to at least two meters.

There are other village trails which are very narrow and ill-defined. However, for tourism growth these trails need to be improved and at some sites rebuilt as mule trails. Development of side trails can be used to entice tourists to stay in the local villages.

Communications

Communications within the Yuksam-Dzongri trek area and to Gangtok is almost nil. Establishment of a wireless set at various locations will help to develop communication in this region. Eventually as traffic increases, reliable communications could be established at Yuksam, Tshoka and Dzongri. It would require a part-time radio operator throughout the trekking season. It is important that all the sites have trailside warning signs or pamphlets at police posts to give detailed information about high altitude sickness, exposure to cold conditions, safety and emergency shelter. The trekking groups should observe safety procedures to combat exposure to bad weather, high altitude and snow blindness.

Campsite Development

Along the Yuksam-Dzongri-Goechha La trekking route, campsites have been recently developed at a few locations by village entrepreneurs. A number of local people in this region are planning to establish campsites in their villages. For the development of campsites and other related facilities, it is suggested to consult and collaborate with Department of Tourism, and the tourist industry, particularly the trekking agencies that have been bringing tourist groups to this area. This association will be responsible for the overall development, maintenance and regular monitoring of campsites, in addition to organizing training and awareness programmes for the campsite owners. Campsites with drinking water and waste disposal facilities are needed.

Lodges and Tourist Facilities

Commercial accommodations are nonexistent in the upper parts of the trek. At that paces tourist huts accommodations are available. But these huts lack clean and proper sanitation facilities. The tourist groups are self-reliant and bring all their supplies, as well as food, from Gangtok. They spend very little money in the local area and buy mainly potatoes and other local vegetables. Recently, a few shops selling tourist goods have opened in the Yuksam village. Shop owners should be encouraged to stock more items and the trekking groups should be kept informed of these.

Trekking will soon increase in the Yuksam-Dzongri trek route. There will be a demand for a substantial number of lodges and restaurants along the trail and in the village which could also be used by groups. These facilities should be developed in a planned and organized way, following a management code that keeps the premises and the surroundings clean and hygienic. Based upon the Sikkim Biodiversity and Ecotourism Project experience, it is advisable to set up lodge management committee in villages. The committee could encourage a local traditional building style, set standards for accommodation, limit the number of lodges and even set food and lodging prices if desirable. The tourism department has to provide strong technical support to the management committees and the village entrepreneurs who want to build and manage lodges. Regular training of lodge owners on hotel management is suggested.

5.8.2. Health and Sanitation

Health and sanitation facilities are not found along the trail and homes are unhygienic. Improvement of health and sanitation must be a top priority if locals are to participate in the tourist business. To improve the health conditions of local people, it is suggested that villages implement sanitation programmes by mobilizing local resources upon the technical advice of Tourism Department. Toilets and proper waste disposal facilities along the trail and in settlement areas should be provided, as well as training facilities for health and sanitation awareness.

5.8.3. Energy

Firewood is the primary source of energy available for cooking purposes although trekking groups carry some kerosene with them, and local people may utilize dried cow dung. Forests close to settlements and trail route have been largely deforested and has become scare even for the local community. The following initiatives are suggested: (i) A medium-to long-term strategy to motivate local people to plant fast growing tree species like alders, pine and spruce in degraded forests; (ii) a number of kerosene depots should be established soon on the trekking route to reduce demand for firewood. These kerosene depots are to be managed by village entrepreneurs who may also choose to sell tourist supplies; and (iii) encourage tour operator to carry small size gas cylinder during trek.

5.8.4. Other Measures

- One of the most important factors in the conservation of the Khangchendzonga Biosphere Reserve is the quality of guides. Instead of the present system, it would be better to trained them with emphasizing an understanding of the special qualities of the KBR and the reasons for the restrict regulations. All guides should require having a basic knowledge of English to ensure communication between tourists. The general control of tourism should be improved. The more attention should be paid the observations and reports of the guides. The scope for new products, such as the use of educational visitor interpretation centers, which introduce visitors to the importance of local culture and history.

- Consider applying for the entire area to be scheduled as a World Heritage Site and implement the site management strategies that this would necessitate. Such a designation would protect the sites, act as a stimulus for high-quality tourism, have considerable publicity value and result in increased tourism revenue.

- Complete a detailed inventory of flora and fauna, their status and also list endangered species for conservation. Biodiversity conservation is a major element for the sustainable development and poverty alleviation and the better livelihood of the nation inparticular in developing countries.All conservation efforts must involve the local people participation.Without the participation of the local people conservation measures may not be successful at all.Because the local people know the nature of the resources of their own locality,through long tradition of resource use, depth knowledge and experiences of wild life and their habitats,and exactly know the way how to protect them, than other people may be outside that locality.

- Like many other national parks, the KBR faces the problem of seasonality especially in reference to foreign tourists. To overcome the problem of seasonality, in this case the tourist season may be extended to whole year by way of several incentives. The other way is to organize special attractions in the off season for example, organizing cultural programmes, and promotional fairs etc. The other method is to consider limiting visitors' number, raising the royalty and implementing a ban on camping based tourism combined with investment in upgrading existing traditional inns to provide unique visitor accommodation. During peak season, a paying guest system may be introduced. This can be done with the co-operation of the local communities, which will enhance their income.

- The higher per capita consumer surplus value and willingness-to-pay by the foreign tourists indicates that an increase in the existing entrance fee for foreign tourists is not likely to affect their visitation rates. Rather, this could generate a considerable income to the park. The foreigners are willing to pay a higher entrance fee and other charges. This will be evident from the income and expenditure pattern of the visitors.
- Improve the existing infrastructure facilities and other facilities like interpretation centre in association with any proposed museum development. Such a centre could brief visitors on the unique social and cultural heritage of the area. Promoting handicrafts to generate more money and employment. Revenue generated from tourism in the park is channeled into the protection and management of the resources.
- Limiting visitor numbers has been exceptionally successful in Bhutan and could be equally so in KBR, but government policy must be clearly established and consistent in order to project an image of a well-managed "quality" industry.
- It was widely proved that local people should be enabled to play a major role in park management and that the appropriate partners for protected area tourism would indeed usually be local communities. This may also offer some compensation for local people, especially if they have been displaced or if their access to resources has been reduced or curtailed. In such circumstances compensation may take the form of capital assistance to develop the tourism venture.
- Protecting socio-cultural values of the area. Keeping in view the rich social and cultural heritage of the region, there should be some special provision to supervise and maintain these traditions.
- Monitoring is a key tool, but one that is properly and frequently used. Monitoring the quality of experience of visitors or the use made of protected areas by local communities should include, and in the following order: identification, analysis for a particular site, placement of this in a regional context and monitoring over time.

- The regulations pertaining to litter and garbage disposal should be enforced more effectively and control of smuggling of NTFPs and butterflies is needed at the airport at Bagdogra.
- Generally the conservation of biodiversity must be given priority through the promotion of ecotourism and the involvement of the local community in all aspects including in decision-making, to ensure the sustainability of tourism in the National Park and also to conserve biodiversity instead of expanding the mass tourism. To achieve this goal, both the Central and State governments should work a lot, and take decisive measures providing economic incentives to local communities that support the biological diversity conservation and that in turn attract and promote ecotourism rather than mass tourism. The Central government in particular should facilitate and attract both national and international organizations and individuals who seek to work on sustainable development, biological diversity conservation and ecotourism in and around the KBR.
- It is proposed that a management plan for the conservation and development of religiocultural resources in the Yuksam region be prepared in consultation with the Department of Archaeology. The participation of Gompa authorities and the local community is vital.

5.8.5. Developing Women's Entrepreneurship in Tourism (DWET)

Mountain tourism is an important potential for income. It has provided job opportunities for thousands of people, particularly through offering scope for diversifying the participation and involvement of women in non-traditional activities. Large numbers of women are involved in the tourism industry. But their employment rate in the direct and formal sectors of the industry is very low, and their involvement is often invisible and unaccounted for. Officially, only 18.8% of the tourism workforce is female (Price, et al. 1997). Yet women's involvement in tourism has been encouraged in few special cases, such as the DWET programme of the Annapurna Conservation Area Project (ACAP) of Nepal.

The DWET programme was launched in 1991 by His Majesty's Government of Nepal, with financial and technical assistance from the UN Development Programme and the International Labour Organization. The programme is specially focused towards developing the entrepreneurial skills of women and training them to use available opportunities.

Table 5.3. Perception of tour operators on compliance of Code of Conduct (%)

Code of Conduct	Strongly agreed	Agreed	Neutral	Disagreed	Strongly disagreed
1. Conserve Sikkim's natural and cultural heritage					
Do not trample high altitude vegetation, do not pick any flowers or medicinal plants	27	33	15	15	10
Do not disturb wildlife or its habitat	21	30	15	24	10
Do not allow clients to purchase endangered animal parts or antique cultural artifacts	58	21	18	3	-
Support local conservation efforts and income generation activities	43	18	27	12	-
2. Avoid use of fuelwood; use alternative fuels					
Use kerosene, L.P.G. (or other non-wood fuel) for all purpose by all the group members	12	27	27	31	3
Discourage campfires, encourage camp fun	-	13	10	46	3
Follow safely rules when carrying, storing and using kerosene and gas	7	21	30	39	3
3. Leave all camps and trail clean					
Dispose of litter and all non-biodegradable materials	3	10	6	42	39
Use toilet tents on all treks in an environmentally friendly manner	10	21	6	45	18
Use established campsites and avoid trenching around tents	6	18	3	24	49
4. Practice conservation					
Avoid fuel-consumptive menu items, e.g., packed foods and large menu selections	10	15	30	24	21

Table 5.3. (Continued)

Code of Conduct	Strongly agreed	Agreed	Neutral	Disagreed	Strongly disagreed
Re-package food into reusable plastic containers to reduce wastes	6	18	9	24	43
Reduce waste by disposing and repacking also	-	12	42	46	-
5. Practice proper hygiene and sanitation					
Teach all staff about personal hygiene, sanitary, kitchen and camp routines	3	33	15	34	15
Properly treat the drinking water and uncooked vegetables for clients	12	45	33	10	-
Dispose of washing and bathing water well away from streams, use biodegradable soaps	4	33	15	33	15
6. Take responsibility for staff and porter welfare					
Provide adequate warm clothing and other essentialities	3	18	10	69	-
Periodically train staff in first aid, guide responsibilities and sanitation etc.	6	24	7	45	18
7. Properly brief clients before leaving on a trek					
Address cultural do's and don'ts	3	18	9	70	-
Plan days for proper altitude acclimatization	7	24	6	45	18

Source: Maharana, 2000

Table 5.4. Components and responsibility for sustainable tourism

Components of responsible tourism	Travel Agents and Tour Operator	Government Authorities	Lodge/hotels and Restaurants	Local Community	Tourists
Information for the tourists	Encourage code of conduct that respects the wildlife and culture in the destination	Provide information about the area's natural and cultural values	Provide information on public transport and complementary activities	Organize activities that provide a chance to get to know local values	Find out about local values and problems
Safeguard Destination	Guides are well acquainted with natural values and local environmental problems	Area planning follows environmental criteria and respects the architectural heritage	Carry out environmental impact studies; put restoration before new construction	Plan activities so that they do not have a negative impact	Choose offers that do not have an environmental impact; do not expect star facilities
Maintain Biodiversity	Destinations whose biodiversity is threatened or vulnerable are not offered	Protect and signpost valuable on vulnerable areas	Buildings and grounds are planned to blend with landscape	Always avoid risking disturbance or damage	Respect animals and plants; do not buy them as souvenirs
Culture	Guides have a good knowledge of the culture and religion of the host place	Maintain cultural identity; plan tourism so that it benefits all local residents	Provide comfort in keeping with local living standards; offer traditional food	Help integrate tourists in the local way of life	Meet the local population; buy traditional arts and crafts

Table 5.4. (Continued)

Components of responsible tourism	Travel Agents and Tour Operator	Government Authorities	Lodge/hotels and Restaurants	Local Community	Tourists
Save Energy	The visits on offer are nearby and/or accessible by public transport and encourage alternative for fuelwood	Facilitate public transport rather than motor cars; protect pedestrian areas	Adopt energy saving measures and encourage clients to collaborate	Avoid activities that consume fossil fuels	Use public transport, trek, discharge campfires, encourage alternatives to fuelwood
Save Water	Destinations with problems of water shortage or purification are not offered	Install treatment plants and promote economy measures	Install economy mechanisms and encourage clients to collaborate	Avoid activities that squander water or that have an impact on water resources	Save water and avoid wasteful activities
Solid Waste	Advertising leaflets; use recycled paper; provide solid waste disposals	Organize selective collection and recycling; carry out awareness campaigns	Reduce the use of non-recyclable materials	Use equipment and materials that do not generate waste	Avoid non-recyclable containers; always use litter baskets

Source: Rai, 2002

It encourages and assists the trainees to initiate new business or improve the profitability of existing female-owned ventures. This programme is first 'of its kind in entire Hindu-kush Himalayan region to specifically and deliberately target women, was carefully designed to allow women to fully participate in tourism-related enterprises. More than 200 women have directly benefited from the programme which, together with ACAP's gender-related activities, has enabled women to own and manage enterprises, and empowered them both economically and socially (Price, et al. 1997). Although the DWET programme has succeeded in making tourism enterprises more accessible to the women of the ACAP region, it has some shortcomings. For women with no experience or technical skills, this lack of linkages with other aspects of tourism development has hindered them from starting enterprises in new areas. But due to some shortcomings, this is good approach to involve women in tourism sector.

5.8.6. Action Plan for the Near Future

Improvement of tourist facilities such as: (i) Trail improvement in critical sites; (ii) Repair and maintenance of bridges; (iii) Campsite development; (iv) Training and Management- lodges, teas shops; (v) Small-scale cottage industries; (vi) Awareness campaign: hygiene and sanitation; (vii) Energy: kerosene depot, tree planting for firewood.

REFERENCES

Abelson P. (1979) *Cost Benefit Analysis and Environmental Problems*. London, U.K: Saxon House,

Adams, V. (1992) *Tourism and Sherpa, Nepal: reconstruction of reciprocity.* Annals of Tourism Research, 19: 534-554.

Anonymous (1997) *Tourism Master Plan of Sikkim, 1997-2011*. Department of Tourism, Government of Sikkim.

Arrow K. J., Solow R., Portney P. R., Leamer E. E., Radner R., Schuman H. (1993) *Report on the National Oceanic and Atmospheric Administration (NOAA) panel on contingent valuation*. Federal Register, 58 (10): 4601-4614.

Ashley, C. and Roe, D. (1998) *Enhancing Community Involvement in Wildlife Tourism.* IIED Wildlife and Development, Serial No. 11.

Banskota, K. and Upadhyay, M. (1991) *Impact of Rural Tourism on Environment, Income, and Employment: Implications for Tourism Development in the Makalu-Barun Conservation Area.* Makalu-Barun Conservation Project, Kathmandu, Nepal.

Bateman, I. J., Cole, M. A., Georgiou, S., Hadley, D. J. (2006) *Comparing contingent valuation and contingent ranking: a case study considering the benefits of urban river water quality improvements.* Journal of Environmental Management, 79 (3): 221-231.

Bateman, I.J., Carson, R.T., Day, B., Hanemann, M., Hanley, R. and Hett, T. (2002) *Economic Valuation with Stated Preference Techniques: A Manual.* Edward Elgar, Northampton, MA.

Binter, M. J. and Booms, B. H. (1982) *Trends in travel and tourism marketing: the changing structure of distribution channels.* Journal of Travel Research, 20 (4): 39-44.

Bishop R. C., Heberlin, T. A. (1995) *The contingent valuation method.* In: Natural Resource Damages: Law and Economics, Ward K.M. and Duffiled, J.W. (eds.). John Willey and Sons, New York, USA, pp 281-309.

Boo, E. (1990) *Ecotourism: The Potential and Pitfalls.* World Wide Fund, Washington, DC, USA.

Boyd, S. W., Butler, R. W., Haider, W., and Perera, A. (1994) *Identifying areas for ecotourism in Northern Ontario: application of a Geographical Information System methodologies.* Journal of Applied Recreation Research, 19: 11-66.

Bridgewater, P. B., Walton, D. W., Busby, J. R. and Reville, B. J. ed. (1992) *Theory and practice in framing a national system for conservation in Australia.* Australian Nature Conservation Agency, Canberra.

Brockelman, W. Y. (1988) *The role of nature trekking in conservation.* International Symposium on Nature Conservation and Tourism Development. Sturat Thai, Thailand, August 22-25 (mimeo).

Brookfield, H. C. (1988) *Sustainable development and the environment.* Journal of Development Studies, 25:126-135.

Brookshire, D., Eubanks, L. S. and Randall, A. (1983) *Estimating option prices and existence values for wildlife resources.* Land Economics, 59: 1-15

Brown, K., Turner, R.K., Hameed, H., and Bateman, I. (1997) *Environmental carrying capacity and tourism development in the Maldives and Nepal.* Environmental Conservation, 24 (4): 116- 225.

Bryden, J. and Faber, M. (1971) *Multiplying the tourist multiplier.* Social and Economic Studies, 20 (1): 68

Buckley, R. (2004) *The effects of world heritage listing on tourism to Australian National Park.* Journal of Sustainable Tourism, 12:70-84.

Budowski, G. (1976) *Review of the Sociological Literature on Tourism.* World Bank, New York.

Butler, J.R. (1992) *Ecotourism: its changing face and evolving philosophy.* Paper Presented in IV World Congress on Natural Parks and Protected Areas, 10-21 February, Caracas, Venezuela.

Ceballos-Lascuráin,H. (1988) *The future of ecotourism.* Mexico Journal, 17: 13-14.

Ceballos-Lascurain, H. (1993) *Ecotourism in Central America.* Technical Report for WTO/UNDP Project CAM 790/011.

Ceballos-Lascurian, H. (1996) *Tourism, Ecotourism and Protected Areas.* IUCN,GLAND, Switzerland.

Chape, S., Blyth, S., Fox, P., and Spalding, M. (2003) *United Nations List of Protected Areas.* IUCN, Gland, Switzerland and Cambridge, UK, and UNEP-WCMC, Cambridge, UK.

Chettri, N., Sharma, E., Deb, D.C. and Sundriyal, R.C. (2002) *Impact of firewood extraction on tree structure, regeneration and woody biomass productivity in a trekking corridor of the Sikkim Himalaya.* Mountain Research and Development, 22 (2): 150-158.

Choi, A. S., Ritchie, B. W., Papandrea, F. and Bennett, J. (2010) *Economic valuation of cultural heritage sites: a choice modeling approach.* Tourism Management, 31: 213-220.

Christ, C., Hillal, O., Matus, S. and Sweeting, J. (2003) *Tourism and Biodiversity: Mapping Tourism Global Footprint.* UNEP, Conservation International (CI), Washington, DC, USA.

Cicia, G. and Scarpa, R. (2000) *Willingness to pay for Rural Landscape Preservation: A Case Study in Mediterranean Agriculture.* Nota di lavoro No 59, Fondazion Eni Enrico Mattei, Milano.

Ciriacy-Wantrup, S.V. (1947) *Capital returns from soil-conservation practices.* Journal of Farm Economics, 29: 1188-1190.

Conservation International (2005) CIFACTS. *Biodiversity Hotspots.* www. conservation.org.

Cordell H.K., Bergstrom J.C. (1993) *Comparison of recreation use values among alternative reservoir water level management scenarios.* Water Resource Research, 29: 247-258.

Costanza, R., d Arge, R., De Groot, R., Farber, S., Grasso, M., Hannon, B., Limburg, K., Naeem, S., O Neill, R.V., Paruelo, J., Raskin, R.G., Sutton, P. And Van den Belt, M. (1997) *The value of the world's ecosystem services and natural capital.* Nature, 387: 253-260.

Cummings R.G., Brookshire D.S., Schulze W.D. eds. (1986) *Valuing Environmental Goods: An Assessment of the Contingent Valuation Method.* Totown, Rowman and Alanheld, NJ, USA.

Dale, H. E. (1999) *Ecological Economics and the Ecology of Economics.* Edward Elgar, Cheltenham, U.K.

Davis, R. (1963) *The Value of Outdoor Recreation: An Economic Study of the Maine Woods.* Doctoral Dissertation in Economics, Harvard University, Cambridge, MA.

Eagles, P. (2001) *International trends in park tourism.* Paper for Federation of Nature and National Parks of Europe.

Ehrlich, P.R. and Wilson, E.O. (1991) *Biodiversity studies: Science and policy.* Science, 253: 758-762.

ESDWG (1991) *Ecological Sustainable Development Working Group,* 1991, Australia.

Flint, M. (1992) *Biological diversity and developing countries.* In: The Earthscan Reader in Environmental Economics, (eds.) Markandya, A. and Richardson, J. Earthscan, London.

Fomenko G.A., Fomenko M.A., Markandya A., Perelet R. (1997) *Natural Resource Accounting for the Oblast of Yaroslavl in the Russian Federation.* Environment Discussion Paper No. 35, NIS-EEP Project. Harvard Institute for International Development, Cambridge, MA.

Fravar, M.T. and Glaeser, B. (1979) *Politics of Ecodevelopment.* Berlin International Institute of Environment and Society, Germany.

Freeman, A. M. III (1993) *The Measurement of Environmental and Resource Values: Theory and Methods.* Resources for the Future, Washington, DC.

Friedmann, J., Wheelwright, E. and Connel, J. (1980) *Development Strategies in the Eighties.* Development Studies, University of Sydney, Sydney, Colloquium.

Garrod G. D. and Willis K. G. (1999) *Economic Valuation of the Environment: Method and Case Studies.* Edward Elgar, Cheltenham.

Gaston, K.J. (1998) *Biodiversity.* Blackwell Science, Oxford.

Gibbs, W. (2001) *On the termination of species.* Scientific American, 285: 40-49.

Gosling, S. (1999) *Ecotourism: A means to safeguard biodiversity and ecosystem functions.* Ecological Economics, 29:303-320.

Green, M. J. B., and Paine, J. (1997) *State of the world's protected areas at the end of the twentieth century.* Paper presented at IUCN World Commission on Protected Areas Symposium on "Protected Areas in the 21st. Century: From Islands to Networks", Albany,Australia, 24-29 November, 1997.

Groth, A. (2000) *Sustainable tourism and the environment.* International Science, Technology and Environmental Education Newsletter, xxv, 1-2.

Hadker N., Sharma S., David A., Muraleedharan T. R. (1997) *Willingness-to-pay for Borvli National Park: evidence from a contingent valuation.* Ecological Economics, 21(2): 105-122.

Hameed, H. (1993) *Sustainable Tourism in Maldives.* M. Phil. dissertation, University of East Anglia, Norwich, U.K.

Hanemann W. M., Loomis J., Kanninen B.J. (1991) *Statistical efficiency of double bounded dichotomous choice contingent valuation.* American Journal of Agricultural Economics, 73: 1255-1263.

Hanley, N. and Spash (1993) *Cost-Benefit Analysis and the Environment.* Edward Elgar, Aldershot.

Hanneman W. M. (1994) *Valuing the environment through contingent valuation.* Journal of Economic Perspectives, 8: 19-43.

Hansen, B., Trine, H.C. and Wanhill, S. (1998) *The economic evaluation of cultural and heritage projects: conflicting methodologies.* Tourism, Culture and Communication, 1 (1):27-48.

Hansen, A.J., DeFries, and Turner, W. (2004) *Land use change and biodiversity: a synthesis of rates and consequences during the period of satellite imagery, pp 277-299.* In: Land Change Science: Observing, Monitoring, and Understanding Trajectories of Change on the Earth's Surface, (eds.) Gutman, G. and Justice, G. Kluwer Academic Publishers, New York.

Heberlein J.A. (1988) *Economics and social psychology in amenity valuation.* In: Amenity Resource Valuation: Integrating Economics with other Disciplines, (eds.) Peterson, G.L., Driver, B.L., Gregory, R. Venture Publishing Inc., State College, PA, USA, pp 235-244.

Hinrichsen, D., Lucas, P.H. and Upreti, B.N. (1983) *Saving Sagarmatha.* Ambio, 12: 203-205.

Hufschmidt M. M., James D. E., Meister A. D., Bower B. T., Dixon J. A. (1983) *Environmental, Natural Systems and Development: An Economic Valuation Guide.* Johns Hopkins University Press, Baltimore, MD, USA.

Hvenegaard, G.T. (1994) *Ecotourism: a status report and conceptual framework.* The Journal of Tourism Studies, 5 (2): 24-35.

IUCN *(International Union for Conservation of Nature and Natural Resources) (1993) United Nations List of Protected Areas.* Prepared by WCMC and WCPA. IUCN, Gland, Switzerland.

IUCN *(International Union for Conservation of Nature and Natural Resouces) (1998) 1997United Nations List of Protected Areas. Prepared by WCMC and WCPA. IUCN,* Gland, Switzerland and Cambridge, UK. 1xii + 412pp.

Jain, S. K. and DeFilipps (1991) *Medicinal Plants of India, Volumes 1-2.* Reference Publications, Michigan.

Karan, P. P. and Mather, C. (1985) *Tourism and environment in Mount Everest Region.* Geographical Review, 75 (1): 93-95.

Kayastha, S. L. (1973) *Editorial Notes.* National Geographical Journal of India, Vol. XIX: 82.

Keating, M. (1993) *The Earth Summit's Agenda for Change.* Centre for Our Common Future, Geneva, Switzerland.

Kenchington, R. A. (1989) *Tourism in the Golapagos Islands: the dilemma of conservation.* Environmental Conservation, 16 (3): 227-236.

Khoshoo, T. N. (1992) *Plant Diversity in the Himalaya: Conservation and Utilization.* II Pandit Gobind Ballabh Pant Memorial Lecture, Gangtok.

Khoshoo, T. N. (1996) *Biodiversity in the Indian Himalayas: Conservation and utilization.* In: Banking on Biodiversity, Sheggi, P. (ed.). International Centre for Integrated Mountain Development, Kathmandu.

Kluvankova T. (1999) *Sustainable tourism in the Mala Fatra National Park, The Slovak Republic.* International Journal of Sustainable Development, 2 (2): 323-340.

Kaminski, J., McLoughlin, J. and Sodagar, B. (2007) *Economic methods for valuing European cultural heritage sites (1994-2006).* In: Perspectives on Impact, Technology and Strategic Management,Vol. I pp98-112., (eds.) McLoughlin, J., Kaminski, J. and Sodagar, B.. EPOCH, Budapest.

Kneese A. (1984) *Measuring the Benefits of Clean Air and Water.* Resource for the Future, Washington, DC, USA.

Knoll, A. H. (1984) *Patterns of extinction in the fossil record of vascular plants.* In: Extinction, Netecki, B.H. (ed.). University of Chicago Press, Chicago.

Kothari, et. al., (1989) *Building Bridge for Conservation: Towards Joint Management of Protected Areas in India.* IAPA, New Delhi.

Lachungpa, U. (1998) *Faunal diversity in Sikkim: an overview.* In: Sikkim: Perspective for Planning and Development, (eds.) Rai, S.C., Sundriyal, R. C. and Sharma, E. Bishen Singh and Mahendra Pal Singh, Dehra Dun.

Laitila, T., and Paulrud, A. (2006) *A multi-attribute extension of discrete-choice contingent valuation for valuation of angling site characteristics.* Journal of Leisure Research, 38 (2): 133-142.

Lawson, F. and Baud-Bovy, M. (1977) *Tourism and Recreation Development.* CBI. Pub. Com. Inc.

Lepcha, G. (1998) *Khangchendzonga Biosphere Reserve.* In: Biosphere Reserves and Management in India, (eds.) Maikuri, R. K., Rao, K. S. and Rai, R. K.. Himavikas Occassional Publication No. 12, G.B. Pant Institute of Himalayan Environment and Development, Almora, India.

Lette, H. and de Boo, H. (2002) *Economic Valuation of Forests and Nature: A support Tool for Effective Decision-making.* Theme Study No. 6, EC-LNV, Ede.

Lindberg, K. and Hawkins, D.E., ed. (1993) *Ecotourism: A Guide for Planners and Managers.* The Ecotourism Society, North Bennington, Vermont, USA.

Lindberg, K., Enriquez, J. and Sproule, K. (1996) *Ecotourism questioned: case study from Belize.* Annals of Tourism Research, 23: 543-562.

Loomis, J.B and Ekstand, E. (1998) *Alternative approach for incorporating respondent uncertainty when estimating willingness to pay the case of the Mexican spotted Owl.* Ecological Economics, 27: 29-41.

Lovejoy, T. E. (1980a) *Conservation Biology: An evolutionary-ecological perspective,V-IX.* Sinauer Associates, Suderland, USA.

Lovejoy, T. E. (1980b) *Changes in Biological Diversity. The Global 2000 report to the president.* Vol. 2 (the technical report), Penguin Books, USA.

Maharana, I. (2000) *Economic Benefits and Conservation Linkages from Tourism Development in the Sikkim Himalaya.* Ph.D. Thesis, North Bengal University, Darjeeling District, West Bengal, India.

Maharana, I., Rai S.C., Sharma E. (2000) *Environmental economics of the Khangchendzonga National Park in the Sikkim Himalaya, India.* Geojournal, 50: 329-337.

Maiti, A. and Chauhan, A.S. (1999) *Threatened plants in the Sikkim Himalaya.* Himalayan Paryavaran, 113-120.

Majid, I., Sinden, J.A., and Randell, A. (1983) *Benefit evaluation increments to existing system of public facilities.* Land Economics, 59: 377-392.

Malhotra, R. K. (1998) *Economic Dimensions of Tourism.* Anmol Publications Pvt. Ltd., New Delhi.

Manoharan, T.R. (1996) *Economics of Protected Areas: A Case Study of Periyar Tiger Reserve.* Ph.D. Thesis, Forest Research Institute, Dehradun.

McKean, P. F. (1989) *Towards a theoretical analysis of tourism: economic dualism and cultural involution.* In: Hosts and Guest: The anthropology of tourism, (ed).V.L. Smith, pp.119-136.   University of Pennsylvania Press, Philadelphia.

McLaren, D. (1993) *Ecotourism: A Growing Consciousness is Change the Tourism Industry.* Earthwise Travel, Washington, DC.

McNeely, J. (1993) *Economic incentive for conserving biodiversity.* Lessons from Africa. Ambio, 22(2-3):147-150.

McNeely, J. A. (1988) *Economics and Biological Diversity: Developing and Using Economic Incentives to Conserve Biological Resources.* IUCN, Switzerland.

McNeely, J. A., Miller, K. R., Reid, W. Mittermeier, R. and Werner, T. (1990) *Conserving the World's Biological Diversity.* IUCN, WRI, World Bank, WWF-US, CI, USA.

MEA (Millennium Ecosystem Assessment) (2005a) *Ecosystems and Human Well-being.* World Resource Institute, Washington DC, www.wri.org

MEA (Millennium Ecosystem Assessment) (2005b) *Ecosystems and Human Well-being: Desertification Synthesis.* World Resource Institute, Washington DC, www.wri.org

Miller, S. E. (1993) *Biological Collections databases available on Internet.* Pacific Science Association Bulletin 45:14-15.

Mitchell R. C., Carson R. T. (1989) *Using Surveys to Value Public Goods: The Contingent Valuation Method. Resources for the Future, Washington, DC, USA.*

MOEF *(Ministry of Environment and Forests)* (1999) Annual Report (1999-2000). Ministry of Environment and Forests, New Delhi.

Moons, E. (2003) *The Development and Application of Economic Valuation Techniques and Their Use in Environmental Policy:* A Survey. Working Paper No. 7, Faculty of Economics and Applied Economic Sciences, Leuven.

Mullarkey, D. J., Bishop, R. C. (1995) *Toward assessing the validity of contingent valuation in Wetlands.* In: Sustaining Coastal Resources: Economics and Natural Sciences, (ed.) Colgan C. S. University of Southern Maine, Portland, Main, Portland, USA, pp57-85.

Munasinghe, M. (1992) *Biodiversity protection policy: environmental valuation and distribution issue.* Ambio, 21: 227-236.

Munasinghe, M. (1993) *Environmental economics and biodiversity management in developing countries.* Ambio, 22 (2-3): 126-135.

Murthy, M. N. and Menkhaus, S. M. (1994) *Economic Aspects of Wldlife Protection in the Developing Countries: A Case Study of Keolado National Park, Bharatpur, India.* Working Paper Series No. E/163/94. Institute of Economic Groth, Delhi University Enclave, Delhi.

Navrud, S. (ed) (1992) *Pricing the European Environment.* Scandinavian University Press, Oslo, Norway and Oxford University Press.

Navrud, S., Mungatana, E. D. (1994) *Environmental valuation in developing countries: the recreational value of wildlife viewing.* Ecological Economics, 11: 135-151.

Navrud, S. and Ready, R. C. (eds.) (2002) *Valuing Cultural Heritage: Applying Environmental Evaluation Techniques to Historic Buildings, Monuments and Artefacts.* Edward Elgar, Cheltenham.

Newbery, (1998) *Comment: Tourism-A Tool for Good or Evil?* Orbit No. 69, p. 2, VSO, London.

Nolte, B. (2004) *Sustainable tourism in biosphere reserves of east Central European countries: case studies from Slovakia, Hungary and the Czech Republic.* In: Policies, Methods and Tools for Visitor Mnagement, (eds) Sievane, N. T., Erkkonen, J., Jokimaki, J., Tuuletie, S. and Virtanen, E., pp. 349-356. Rovaniemi: Proceedings of the Second International Conference on Monitoring and Management of Visitors Flows in Recreational and Protected Areas.

Noonan, D. (2003) *Contingent valuation and cultural resources: a meta-analytic review of the literature.* Journal of Cultural Economics, 27:159-176.

Norgard, R. (1984) *Coevolutionary development potential.* Land Economics, 60: 2

Noronha, R. (1976) *Review of the Sociological Literature on Tourism.* World Bank, New York.

Norse, E.A., Rosenbaum, K.L., Wilcove, D.S., Wilcox, B.A., Romme, W.H., Johnston, D.W., and Stout, M.L. (1986) *Conserving Biological Diversity in our Natural Forests*. The Wilderness Society, Washington, USA.

Nunes, P. A. L. D., van den Bergh, J., Nijkamp, P. (2003) *The Ecological Economics of Biodiversity: Methods and Policy Applications*. Edward Elgar, Northampton.

OHC-Scherer, Julia, Elke, Mannigel, Chris, Kirkby, Clenn, H. Shebard, Jr. and Douglas, W. Yu. (2008) *Indigenous ecotourism in Amazon: a case study of "Casa Matsigulenka" Manu National Park*. Environmental conservation, 35(1): 14-25.

Palmer, C. (1999) *Tourism and the symbols of identity*. Tourism Management, 20: 313-321.

Partney, P. R. (1981) *Housing prices, health effects and valuing reductions in risk of death*. Journal of Environmental Economics and Management, 8 (1): 72-78.

Pawson, I. G., Dennyse, D., Stanford, V., Adams, A., and Mingms, N. (1984) *Growth of tourism in Nepal's Everest region: impact on the physical environment and structure of human settlements*. Mountain Research and Development, 4 (3): 237-246.

Pearce, D., Whittington, D. and Georgiou, S. (1994) *Economic Values and the Environment in the Developing world*. A Report on the UNEP.

Pearce, D. W. and Moran, D. (1994) *The Value of Biodiversity*. Earth scan, London.

Plog, S. C. (1972) *Why destination areas rise and fall in popularity. Unpublished paper presented to the Southern California Chapter*. The Travel Research Association.

Pradhan, U. C. (1976) *Indian Orchids: Guide Identification and Culture, Vol. I.*, Primulaceae Books, Kalimpong, India.

Pradhan, U. C. (1979) *Indian Orchids: Guide Identification and Culture, Vol. II.*, Primulaceae Books, Kalimpong, India.

Pradhan, U.C. and Lachungpa, S.T. (1990) *Sikkim Himalayan Rhododendrons*. Primulaceae Books, Kalimpong, India.

Price, M.F., Laurence, A.G.M. and Williams, P.W. (1997) *Tourism and amenity migration, pp 249-280*. In: Mountains of the World: A Global Priority, (eds) Messerli, B. and Ives, J.D. The Parthenon Publishing Group, London.

Rai, R.K. (1998) *Biosphere Reserve: concept, characteristics function and management*. In: Biosphere Reserves and Management in India, (eds.) Maikuri, R.K., Rao, K.S. and Rai, R.K.. Himavikas Occassional Publication

No. 12, G.B. Pant Institute of Himalayan Environment and Development, Almora, India.

Rai, S.C. (2002) *Adventure travel and sustainable tourism management in the Sikkim Himalaya*. In: Recent Advances in Geomorphology, Quarternary Geology and Environmental Geosciences: Indian Case Study, (eds.) Tandon, S.K. and Thakur, B. Manisha Publications, Delhi.

Rai, S.C. and Sundriyal R.C. (1997) *Tourism and biodiversity conservation: The Sikkim Himalaya*. Ambio, 26: 235-242.

Rai, T.D. and Rai, L.K. (1993) *Trees of the Sikkim Himalaya*. Indus Book Publishing Co., New Delhi.

Redcliff, Edward, B. (1992) *A New Context for a System of Indigenious Knowledge*. Kegal Paul, International, London.

Reid, W. V. and Miller, K. R. (1989) *Keeping Options Alive-The Scientific Basis for Conserving Wildlife*. World Resource Institute, Washington, DC.

Rodger, G. (1989) *Ecologically sustainable development in Australian Alps*. Mountain Research and Development, 15 (3): 251-258.

Rodriguez, L. O., and Young, K. R. (2000) *Biological diversity of Peru: determining priority areas for conservation*. Ambio, 29: 329-337.

Sable, K.A. and Kling, R.W. (2001) *The double public good; a conceptual framework for shared experience values associated with heritage conservation*. Journal of Cultural Economics, 25:77-89.

Sala, O. E., Chapin III, F. S., Armesto, J. J., Berlow, R., Bloomfield, J., Dirzo, R., Huber-Sanwald, E., Huenneke, L. F., Jackson, R. B., Kinzig, A., Leemans, R., Lodge, D., Mooney, H. A., Oesterheld, M., Poff, N. L., Sykes, M. T., Walker, B. H., Walker, M., and Wall, D. H. (2000) *Global biodiversity scenarios for the year 2100*. Science, 287: 1770-1774.

Schlapfer, F. (2006) *Survey protocol and income effects in the contingent valuation of public goods: a meta-analysis*. Ecological Economics, 57 (3): 415-429.

Shackley, M. (1999) *Trekking tourism in Peru: the case of the Inca trail*. Unpublished paper.

Signor, P.W. (1990) *The geological history of diversity*. Annual Review of Ecology and Systematics, 21: 509-539.

Singh, J. S. and Singh, S. P. (1987) *Forest vegetation of the Himalaya*. Boatnical Review, 53: 80-192.

Singh, J. S. and Singh, S. P. (1992) *Forest of Himalaya*. Gyanodaya Prakashan, Nainital, India.

Singh, J. S., Singh, S. P. and Gupta, S. R. (2006) *Ecology, Environment and Resource Conservation*. Anamaya Publishers, New Delhi.

Singh, P. and Chauhan, A.S. (1998) *An overview of plant diversity of Sikkim Himalaya.* In: Sikkim: Perspective for Planning and Development, (eds.) Rai, S.C., Sundriyal, R..C. and Sharma, E. Bishen Singh and Mahendra Pal Singh, Dehra Dun.

Singh, S.N. (1986) *Geography of Tourism and Recreation.* Inter-India Publication, New Delhi.

Sreedhar, R. (1995) *Mountain Tourism for Local Community Development: A Report on Case Study in Kinnaur District, H.P. and Badrinath;* Series No. MEI 95/13, ICIMOD, Kathmandu, Nepal.

Sreedhar, R. (1995a) *Mountain Tourism in Himachal Pradesh and the Hill District of Uttar Pradesh: An Overview.* Discussion Paper, Series No. MEI/95/6. ICIMOD, Kathmandu, Nepal.

Sreedhar, R. (1995b) *Mountain Tourism for Local Community Development: A Report on Case Study in Kinnaur District, H.P. and Badrinath Tourist Zone, U.P.* Discussion Paper Series No. MEI/95/13. ICIMOD, Kathmandu, Nepal.

Stanton, N. L. and Lattin, J. D. (1989) *In defense of species.* Bioscience, 36: 368-373.

Stevens, S., Sherpa, M.N. and Sherpa, L.N. (1989) *Tourism and Local Development in Sagarmatha National Park*, Nepal, Manuscript.

Sundriyal R.C. and Sharma, E. (1996) *Anthropogenic pressure on tree structure and biomass in the temperate forest of Mamlay watershed in Sikkim.* Forest, Ecology and Management, 81: 113-134.

Sundriyal, M. (1999) *Distribution, Propagation and Nutritive Value of Some Wild Edible Plants in the Sikkim Himalaya.* Ph.D. Thesis, HNB Garhwal University, Srinagar.

Sundriyal, R.C., Sharma, E., Rai, L.K. and Rai, S.C. (1994) *Tree structure, regeneration and woody biomass removal in a sub-tropical forest of Mamlay watershed in the Sikkim Himalaya.* Vegetatio, 113: 53-63.

Tadesse, B. (2009) *Biodiversity Conservation and Ecotourism in Semen Mountains National Park, Ethiopia.* Unpublished Ph.D. Thesis, University of Delhi, Delhi.

Throsby, D. (2001) *Economics and Culture.* Cambridge University Press, Cambridge, UK.

Tamang, P. (1993) *Fish Fauna and River Systems in Sikkim.* Ph.D. Thesis, Guwahati University, Assam.

Taylor, J.E., Dyer, G.A., Stewart, M., Yunez-Naude, A., and Ardila, S. (2003) *The economics of ecotourism: a Galapagos Island, economic -wide perspective.* Economic Development and Cultural Change, 51, 977-997.

Trekking Master Plan for Sikkim (2000) *Department of Tourism,* Government of Sikkim.

UN (1963) U.N. *Recommendation on International Travel and Tourism, Rome.* U.N. Publication Symbol E/CONF/47/18.

Venkatachalam, L. (2004) *The contingent valuation method: a review.* Environmental Impact Assessment Review, 24 (1): 89-124.

Verbic M. (2006) *Analysis of stated preferences as an approach to economic valuation of environmental values and natural and cultural heritage.* IB Review, 40(1-2): 21-36.

Verbic M. and Slabe-Erker R. (2009) *An econometric analysis of willingness-to-pay for sustainable development: a case study of the Volcji Potok landscape.* Ecological Economics, 68: 1316-1328.

W. T. O. (2006) *Year Book of Tourism Statistics ed.* World Trade Organisation Madrid, Spain.

Wallace, G.N. and Pierce, S.M. (1996) *An evaluation of ecotourism in Amazons, Brazil.* Annals of Tourism Research, 23: 843-873.

Walsh, G. (1986) *Recreation Economic Decisions: Comparing Benefits and Costs.* State College, PA, USA: Venture Publishing Inc.

Wells, M. and Brandon, K. (1992) *People and Parks: Linking protected areas management with local communities.* Washington DC: The World Bank, The World Wildlife Fund and US Agency of International Development.

Wells, M., Brandon, K. and Hannah, L. (1990) *People and Parks: An Analysis of Projects Linking Protected Area Management with Local Communities.* Draft Report. The World Bank, Washington, DC, USA.

Whittington, D. (1998) *Administering contingent valuation surveys in developing countries.* World Development, 26 (1): 21-30

Wilson, M. A. and Carpenter, S. R. (1999) *Economic valuation of freshwater ecosystem services in the United States: 1971-1997.* Ecological Applications, 9: 772-283.

Wilson, E.O. (1984) *Biophilia.* Harward University Press, Cambridge, USA.

Wilson, E.O. and Peters, F.M. (eds), (1988) *Biodiversity.* National Academy Press, Washington DC. USA.

Wolfe, R.I. (1952) *Wasanga beach: the diverse from the geographical environment.* The Canadian Geographer, 2: 57-66.

Wood, K. and House, S. (1991*) The Good Tourist: A Worldwide Guide for Green Traveller.* Mandarin, London.

Wood, M.E. (1992) *Ecotourism is tested as global conservation strategy.* The Ecotourism Society Newsletter, Spring/Summer.

Woodroffe, R., and Ginsberg, J.R. (1998) *Edge effects and the extinction of population inside protected areas.* Science, 280: 2126-2128.

World Tourism Organization (1991) *Tourism Growth Around the World.* Madrid (WTO).

World Tourism Organization (1999) *Guide for Local Authorities on Developing Sustainable Tourism.* Supplementary Volume Sub Saharan Africa.

World Tourism Organization (2002) *Tourism and poverty allivation,*WTO, 2002,Madrid.

Wunder, S. (2000) *Ecotourism and economic incentives: an empirical approach.* Ecological Economics, 32, 465-479.

www.propoortourism.org.uk, (2004) *Pro-poor tourism,* Developing countries share of the international tourism market.www.propoortourism.org.uk. 2004.

Yonzon, P. B. and Hunter, M. L. J. (1991) *Chees, tourists and red pandas in the Nepal Himalayas.* Conservation Biology, 5: 196-201.

Ziffer, K. A. (1989) *Ecotourism: The Uneasy Alliance.* Ernst & Young, Washington, DC, USA.

Zimmerer, K.S., Galt, R.E., and Buck, M.V. (2004*) Globalization and multi-spatial trends in the coverage of protected-area conservation (1980-2000).* Ambio, 33: 520-529

Zurik, D.N. (1992) *Adventure tourism and sustainable tourism in the peripheral economy of Nepal.* Annalas, Association of American Geographers, 82: 608-628.

Zurick, D., Pacheco, J., Shrestha, B. and Bajracharya, B. (2005) *Atlas of the Himalaya.* ICIMOD, Kathmandu, Nepal.

Appendix-1. Endangered plants of the Sikkim Himalaya

Botanical Name	Family	IUCN status	Distribution	Habitat	Flowering &Fruiting season	Remarks
			A: Flowering Species			
Acer hookeri Miq. Var. *majus Pax*	Aceraceae	CR	India: Sikkim, West Bengal	In sub-tropical wet forests 600-1500m	October	Known only from type collection by Anderson 1862 (Rinchingpong)
Acer osmastonii Gamble	Aceraceae	CR	India: Darjeeling, West Bengal, Dehra Dun	In wet montane temperate forest 1500-2400m	October	Reported only from small pockets at Birch Hill&Salombong in Darjeeling district
Aconitum ferox Wallich ex Seringe	Ranunculaceae	EN	India: Himachal Pradesh to Sikkim	In temperate to subalpine regions 3300-3500m	July to November	Threatened by overexploitation for medicinal use
Acronema pseudotenera P.K. Mukherjee	Apiaceae	DD	India: Sikkim	On alpine meadows 3500-4200m	July to November	Not collected since 1892
Angelica nubigena (C.B. Clarke, P.K. Mukharjee)	Apiaceae	DD	India: Sikkim	Along open water courses 3800m	July to November	Not collected since 1849
Aphyllorchis parviflora King & Pantling	Orchidaceae	EN	India: Sikkim, Garhwal, Nepal, NE. Tibet	On humus-rich black soils, under canopy of Quercus 3600-3700m	June to July	Known from Yumthang&Lachen in Sikkim, and recently from the Garhwal Himalaya
Arenaria thangoensis Smith	Caryophyllaceae	CR	India: Sikkim, Nepal, S.E. Tibet	In alpine regions with Primula & Rhododendron 4200-4500m	September	Not collected since 1912. Habitat areas subject to heavy summer&post-monsoon grazing

Appendix 1. (Continued)

Botanical Name	Family	IUCN status	Distribution	Habitat	Flowering & Fruiting season	Remarks
			A: Flowering Species			
Aristolochia grifithii Hook.f. &Thomson ex Duch	Aristolochiaceae	VU	India: Sikkim, Nepal, S.E. Tibet	Climber on shrubs 1800-2500m	April to May	Over exploitation & destruction of habitat constitute major threats
Balanophora Involucrata Hook.f.	Balanophoraceae	CR	India: West Himalaya to North-east, Nepal, Bhutan, Pakistan, China	In dense forest 2300-3400m	July to October	Deforestation & loss of habitat constitute major threats
Begonia rubella Buch.-Ham. ex. D. Don	Begoniaceae	CR	India: Sikkim, Nepal	On moist shaded banks 600-1800m	June to September	Known only from type collection
Begonia satrapis C.B.Clarke	Begoniaceae	CR	India: Sikkim, Darjeeling	On moist hill slopes 700-1000m	August	Collected from 1875 to 1914. No collection thereafter, although known locations are well surveyed
Beginia scutala Wallich ex DC	Beginiaceae	DD	India:Sikkim, Darjeeling, Peninsular India, Nepal	In subtropical forests 1000-1500m	September	Collected by Wallich in 1821 and recently reported from Peninsular India
Bulleya yunnanensis Scltr.	Orchidaceae	CR	India: Darjeeling, Arunachal, Bhutan, China	Epiphyte on trees 2000m	June to July	Only few known Himalayan populations. Fast-depleting in the wild because of deforestation

Appendix 1. (Continued)

Botanical Name	Family	IUCN status	Distribution	Habitat	Flowering &Fruiting season	Remarks
			A: Flowering Species			
Calamus inermis T. Anderson ex D.Don	Arecaceae	CR	India : Darjeeling	Along shaded streams & ravines in moist tropical forests 800m	April	Yields commercial quality cane. A few clumps exist now at Latpancher & Kalimpong
Calanthe alpine Hook.f. ex Lindley	Orchidaceae	EN	India: Sikkim, Arunachal,Garhw al,Kumaun, Nepal,Bhutan	Near Streams & Shaded temperate regions 2000-3300m	July to August	Known only from a few scattered populations
Calanthe mannii Hook.f.	Orchidaceae	EN	India:Sikkim, Arunachal, Garhwal and Kumaun, Meghalaya, Nepal, Bhutan	Amidst boulders & rocky streams in shaded subtropical & temperate forests	July to August	Known from a few localities with scattered populations
Carex sahmii Galldyal & Bhattacharya	Cyperaceae	DD	India: Sikkim	Not known	May to June	Inadequately-known species
Ceropegia hookerii C.B. Clarke ex Hook.f.	Asclepiadaceae	EN	India: Sikkim, Nepal, Tibet	In alpine grassy meadows 3000-4000m	June to july	Collected from Zemu valley in 1909 and from Tibet in 1945
Ceropegia lucida Wallich	Asclepiadaceae	CR	India: Sikkim, Assam, Meghalaya, Bangladesh	On river banks 2500-3000m	September to November	All collections of the species date from the 19th century
Cissus spectabilis (Kurz.) Planchon	Vitaceae	CR	India: Sikkim, Darjeeling	In moist forests 200-300m	April	No collection since 1875

Appendix 1. (Continued)

Botanical Name	Family	IUCN status	Distribution	Habitat	Flowering &Fruiting season	Remarks
A: Flowering Species						
Codonopsis affinis Hook.f. & Thomson	Campanulaceae	VU	India: Sikkim, Darjeeling	Temperate regions 1800-3400m	August to October	Generally found in Oak forests
Coelogyne treutleri Hook.f.	Orchidaceae	EX	India: Sikkim	Epiphyte	September to October	No collection after the type collection was made by Treutler in 1875
Cotoneaster slmonsii Hort. ex. Hook.f.	Rosaceae	EN	India: Sikkim	In temperate regions 1600-3200m	October to January	All collections made between 1884 and 1909 (Lachung)
Cyathopus sikkimensis Stapf	Poaceae	CR	India: Sikkim	In temperate regions with rhododendron & Potentilla 2000-3000m	September to December	Found in sparse populations. Loss of habitat has rendered the species very rare
Cycas pechtinata Griff.	Cycadaceae	EN	India: Sikkim, Assam, Manipur, Nepal, Mynmar, Tibet	Subtropical open forest 700-1000m	April to August	Overexploitation & habitat destruction constitute major threats
Cymbidium eburneum Lindley	Orchidaceae	EN	India: East Himalaya & North-east Nepal	Epiphyte or lithophyte in humid forest 1000-1500m	April to June	Overexploitation & habitat destruction constitute major threats
Cymbidium hookerianum Relchb.f.	Orchidaceae	EN	India: Sikkim, Nepal, Tibet	Lithophyte or oplphyte on Quercus spp. 1700-2500m	June to July	Sparse in occurrence although known from Kumaun to East Himalaya

Appendix 1. (Continued)

Botanical Name	Family	IUCN status	Distribution	Habitat	Flowering &Fruiting season	Remarks
			A: Flowering Species			
Cymbidium whiteae King & Pantling	Orchidaceae	CR	India: Sikkim, Nepal, Tibet	Occurs as an epiphyte usually on & rarely on Castanopsis	October to November	Has disappeared from its type-locality (Gangtok) following over exploitation & urbanization pressure. Sporadically occurs around Rumtek
Cypripedum elegans Reichb.f.	Orchidaceae	EN	India: Sikkim, Garhwal, Nepal, Bhutan, S.E. Tibet	In shaded places on open hill slpoes & along streams 3300-4200m	June	Very few scattered populations exist. Over exploitation & loss of habitat have rendered it rare
Cypripedium himalaicum Rolfe	Orchidaceae	EN	India: Sikkim, Garhwal and Kumaun, Nepal, Bhutan, S.E. Tibet	On open hill slopes & subalpine meadows amidst shrubs of cotoneaster & permassia 3000-4300m	July to August	Very few scattered surviving populations exist now. Overexploitation has rendered it rare
Didiciea cunminghamii King & Prain ex King & Pantling	Orchidaceae	CR	India: Sikkim, Garhwal	Sub alpine to alpine region ca. 4000m	July	Collected in Garhwal after the lapse of 70 years since being discovered in Sikkim (Lachen)

Appendix 1. (Continued)

Botanical Name	Family	IUCN status	Distribution	Habitat	Flowering &Fruiting season	Remarks
			A: Flowering Species			
Dioscorea deltoidea Wallich ex Kunth	Dioscoreaceae	VU	India: Himalaya (Kashmir to Assam) Afganistan, China	In tropical to temperate montane regions 1000-3500m	May to July	Exploited for medicinal purposes
(Lindley) Lindley *Diplomeris hirsuta*	Orchidaceae	VU	India: Darjeeling, Kumaun, Arunachal, Bhutan, Nepal	On moist rocks in cool shaded places & liverworts 400-700m	June to August	Natural habitats along roadsides are prone to both landslides & encroachment
Draba stenobotrys Gilg & Schulz	Brassicaceae	CR	India:Sikkim	In alpine meadows on grassy sandy soils 4000-5000m	July to September	Under threat from overgrazing & destruction of habitats
Ephedra gerardiana Wallich var. sikkimensis Stapf	Orchidaceae	EN	India: Sikkim, Nepal, Bhutan India: Sikkim, Nepal, Bhutan	Open alpine slopes 3500-4500m	June to July	Restricted distribution. Exploited for medicinal purposes
Gentiana prainii Burkill	Gentianaceae	CR	India: Himalaya (Kashmir to Assam), Afganistan, China	Alpine meadows 3500-4300m	August to October	Found at two locations in Sikkim
Laegerstroemla minuticarpa Debberm. ex P.C. Kanjillal	Lythraceae	DD	India: Sikkim, Assam	Subtropical forests 1000-1500m	August to October	Collected once from Sikkim by Ribu & Rhomo in 1908
Lactuca cooperii Anthony	Asteraceae	CR	India: Sikkim	Exposed hill slopes & sub-alpine regions ca. 5000m	September	Known only from type collection in 1913

Appendix 1. (Continued)

Botanical Name	Family	IUCN status	Distribution	Habitat	Flowering & Fruiting season	Remarks
			A: Flowering Species			
Livistona jenkinsiana Griff.	Arecaceae	VU	India: Sikkim, Arunachal Meghalaya, Assam	Moist forests upto 1000m	April to June	Only found now in a few selected pockets. Under major threat from overexploitation & deforestation
Lioydia himalensis Royle	Liliaceae	DD	India: Sikkim, Himachal Kashmir, Nepal, Bhutan	On cliff or rocks & gravels amidst moss & grass 3700-3800m	May to August	Occurs sporadically. Only represented by a few collected Himalayan speciemns
Ophiorrhiza lurida Hook.f.	Rubiaceae	VU	India: Sikkim, Darjeeling, Manipur, Tibet, S.W. China	On damp shaded mountain slopes 300-1500m	July to August	Habitat changes have rendered it very rare in India
Paphiopedilum fairrieanum (Lindley) Stein	Orchidaceae	CR	India: Sikkim, Arunachal, Bhutan	In open well drained gravelly areas near streams amidst moss & grass 1400-2200m	October to January	Now restricted to small pockets in Sikkim. Overexploitation & overgrazing have jointly brought about decline of the species
Paphiopedilum venustum (Wallich ex Sims.) Pfitz	Orchidaceae	CR	India: Sikkim, Arunachal, Nepal, Bhutan	In moist shaded areas near water 1400-1700m	December to February	Under major threat from overexploitation & habitat destruction

Appendix 1. (Continued)

Botanical Name	Family	IUCN status	Distribution	Habitat	Flowering &Fruiting season	Remarks
			A: Flowering Species			
Panax pseudo ginseng Wallich	Araliaceae	LR	India: E. Himalaya, Tibet, China, Myanmar	On humus-rich soils in dense temperate conifer, oak & birch forest 2900-4000m	May to July	Species of medicinal importance. Found at scattered locations in the Sikkim Himalaya
Phoenix rupicola T. Anderson	Arecaceae	VU	India: Sikkim, Darjeeling, Arunachal Meghalaya	In rocky clefts below 450m	May to June	Exploited for its edible stem-core
Picrorrhiza scrophulariflora Pennel.	Scrophulariceae	CR	India: Sikkim, Nepal, Bhutan, S.W. China	Rocky alpine slopes 3300-5000m	June to September	Suffers from overexploitation as a substitute for Gentiana Kurroo
Pimpinellatongloensis P.K. Mukherjee	Apiaceae	CR	India: Sikkim	Temperate forests 1600-1700m	August to October	Not collected after 1857 & 1868
Pimpinella wallichii C.B. Clarke	Apiaceae	CR	India: Sikkim, Nepal	Subtropical forests 1400-1500m	July to September	Not collected after 1868
Podophyllum hexandrum Royle	Podophyllaceae	EN	India: Sikkim, Arunachal, Meghalaya, Assam	Moist forests	April to June	Only found now in a few selected pockets. Under major threat from overexploitation & deforestation

Appendix 1. (Continued)

Botanical Name	Family	IUCN status	Distribution	Habitat	Flowering &Fruiting season	Remarks
			A: Flowering Species			
Plemopetalum radiatum (W.M. Smith) P.K. Mukherjee	Apiaceae	CR	India: Sikkim	Probably an epiphyte on moss-laden trunks of rhododendron, abies & tsuga 3500m	August to September	No collection since 1892
Rhododendron anthopogon D. Don	Ericaceae	VU	India: Kashmir to Arunachal, S.E. Tibet	Alpine region 3000-5000m	May to June	Exploited for medicinal purpose & also for use as incense
Rhododendron niveum Hook.f.	Ericaceae	EN	India: Sikkim, Bhutan	In rocky valleys & ridges 3100m	April to May	Subject to habitat destruction. Habitats now conserved by state forest department
Rhododendron setosum D.Don	Ericaceae	VU	India: Kashmir to Arunachal, S.E. Tibet	Open rocy alpine region 3000-5000m	June to July	Exploited for medicinal purposes & also for use as incense
Rhopalocnemis phalloides Jung	Balanophoraceae	EN	India: Sikkim, Arunachal, Meghalaya, Indonesia	Found as a root parasite on memebers of Vitaceae family in diffused sunlight on the floors of virgin dense evergreen forests	Decemeber to January	Under threat from loss of host plants & suitable ecological niches

Appendix 1. (Continued)

Botanical Name	Family	IUCN status	Distribution	Habitat	Flowering &Fruiting season	Remarks
			A: Flowering Species			
Swertia chirayita (Roxb. ex Flem.) Karst.	Gentianaceae	CR	India: Kashmir to Sikkim & Meghalaya, Bhutan	Open hill slopes in subtropical & temperate region 1500-2800m	June to July	Threatened by overexploitation for medicinal purposes
Taxus wallichiana Zucc.	Taxaceae	VU	India: Kashmir to Sikkim, Arunachal, Myanmar, China	Temperate hill slopes 2400-2800m	June to November	Of medicinal importance. Restricted distribution in Sikkim
Zeuxina pulchra King & Pantling	Orchidaceae	CR	India: Sikkim, Meghalaya	Cool shaded places by streams & rivers, usually amidst thick undergrowth 2000-2500m	August	Not collected from Sikkim since type collection in 1898 (Lachung)
B. Pteridophytes						
Denmstaedtia elwesii (Baker) Bedd.	Denstaedtiaceae	CR	India: Sikkim (Lachen), Tibet	On hill slopes upto ca. 2700m		No collection since 1889, although known locations are well-surveyed
Mecodium levingei (C.B. Clarke) Copel.	Hymeno-phyllaaceae	EN	India: Sikkim (Yuksam & Lachen); China	High altitude fern, growing on moist shaded rocks & trees 2100-2500m		Collected after 1880 from North Sikkim in 1964
Christiopteris tricuspis (Hook.) Christ.	Polypodiaceae	CR	India: Sikkim, Darjeeling	Terrestrial in subtropical & subtemperate forests		No collection since 1900. Probably depleted by deforestation

Appendix 1. (Continued)

Botanical Name	Family	IUCN status	Distribution	Habitat	Flowering &Fruiting season	Remarks
			A: Flowering Species			
Oreopteris ewesii (Barker) Holtt.	Thelypteridaceae	DD	India: Sikkim (Lachen)	On open hill slopes 2700-4200m		Collected from Sikkim in 1985 after the lapse of 100 years
Christella clarkei (Bedd.) Holtt.	Thelypteridaceae	CR	India: Sikkim	Among boulders along streams ca 4000m		Found in a very narrow pocket in the Darjeeling hills
Cylcogramma squamaestipes (C.B. Clarke) Tagawa	Thelypteridaceae	CR	India: Sikkim (Simonbong)	Along streams as forest undergrowth 1500m		Distributional range now very limited. Threatened by deforestation & habitat loss
Metathelypteris decipiens (C.B. Clarke) Ching	Thelypteridaceae	VU	India: Darjeeling, Meghalaya	Along streams as forest undergrowth		Habitat destruction responsible for decline in population

EX= Extinct; EW=Extinct in the wild; CR= Critically Endangered; EN=Endangered; VU=Vulnerable; LR=Lower Risk; DD=Data deficient; NE=Not Evaluated

Source: Maiti, A. and Chauhan, A.S., (1999)

INDEX

F

G

H